PEN PORTRAITS
OF ILLUSTRIOUS
CASTILIANS

MEDIEVAL TEXTS IN TRANSLATION

EDITORIAL DIRECTOR

Thomas F. X. Noble
University of Notre Dame

EDITORIAL BOARD

Geoffrey Koziol
University of California, Berkeley

Carol Lansing
University of California at Santa Barbara

Barbara H. Rosenwein
Loyola University of Chicago

Fernán Pérez de Guzmán

PEN PORTRAITS OF ILLUSTRIOUS CASTILIANS

translated with introduction and notes
by Marie Gillette and Loretta Zehngut

The Catholic University of America Press
Washington, D.C.

Copyright © 2003
The Catholic University of America Press
All rights reserved

The paper used in this publication meets the minimum requirements of American National Standards for Information Science—Permanence of Paper for Printed Library materials, ANSI Z39.48-1984.
∞

Library of Congress Cataloging-in-Publication Data
Pérez de Guzmán, Fernán, 1376 ?–1460 ?
[Generaciones y semblanzas. English]
Pen portraits of illustrious castilians / Fernán Pérez de Guzmán; Translated, with introduction and notes, by Marie Gillette and Loretta Zehngut.
p. cm. — (Medieval texts in translation)
Includes bibliographical references and index.
ISBN 0-8132-1325-8 (cloth : alk. paper) — ISBN 0-8132-1326-6 (paper : alk. paper)
1. Castile (Spain)—Biography. 2. Castile (Spain)—History.
I. Title. II. Series.
DP136 .P3513 2003
946'.3—dc21

*In the memory
of our beloved parents*

*Peter and Helen Gillette
Tom and Ellen Donahue*

CONTENTS

INTRODUCTION, ix

    Historical Background, ix
    Fernán Pérez de Guzmán: The Author and His Works, xxiv
    About This Work, xxvi
    Manuscript Tradition of *Generaciones y Semblanzas*, xxix
    Translators' Note, xxxi
    Map of Late Medieval Spain, xxxiii
    Genealogical Table of the Kings of Castile and León, xxxiv

PEN PORTRAITS OF
ILLUSTRIOUS CASTILIANS, 1

    Author's Prolog, 3
    King Enrique III, 7
    Queen Catalina, 12
    King Fernando I of Aragón, 12
    Don Ruy López Dávalos, 17
    Don Alfonso Enríquez, 19
    Don Pedro López de Ayala, 20
    Don Diego López de Stúñiga, 21
    Don Diego Hurtado de Mendoza, 22
    Don Gonzalo Núñez de Guzmán, 24
    Don Juan García Manrique, 26
    Don Juan de Velasco, 27
    Don Sancho de Rojas, 28

Don Pedro Tenorio, 28
Don Juan Alfonso de Guzmán, 30
Don Gómez Manrique, 30
Don Lorenzo Suárez de Figueroa, 31
Don Juan González de Avellaneda, 32
Don Pedro Afán de Ribera, 32
Don Garci González de Herrera, 33
Don Juan Hurtado de Mendoza, 33
Don Diego Fernández de Córdoba, 34
Don Álvar Pérez de Osorio, 34
Don Pedro Suárez de Quiñones and
 Don Diego Fernández de Quiñones, 35
Don Pedro Manrique, 37
Don Diego Gómez de Sandoval, 38
Don Pablo, Bishop of Burgos, 39
Don Lope de Mendoza, 43
Don Enrique de Villena, 44
Don Gutierre of Toledo, 46
Don Fernán Alfonso de Robles, 46
Don Pedro, Count of Trastámara, 49
Don Pedro de Frías, 50
King Juan II, 51
Don Álvaro de Luna, 62

Appendix: Personal Titles Used in This Translation, 75

Works Consulted, 79

Index of Persons Mentioned in the Text, 81

INTRODUCTION

Historical Background

Pen Portraits describes a time of conflict in Castilian politics—conflict that was in the making years before it became manifest in the turbulence and social unrest of the early fifteenth century. The hundred-year period from 1350 to 1450 was marked by political, economic, social, and intellectual change throughout Europe: the Hundred Years War, the Papal Schism, the decimation of the population due to the Black Death. Spain did not escape the turbulence, but in spite of it, both the Kingdoms of Aragón and Castilla continued their economic expansion. Aragón looked to the Mediterranean to further its interests, while Castilla directed its energies to the north, strengthening its wool export to the Low Countries.

In both Kingdoms there were disputes over the succession to the throne, and in both Kingdoms nobles challenged the power of the monarchy. Intermarriage among the various royal houses was very common. Illegitimate or younger sons of princely families were exiled or fled to other kingdoms in search of support. Disputes erupted among members of regency councils appointed to govern during the minority of the legitimate monarch. Kings, nobles, and representative assemblies sought to increase their power. All of these factors led to a bloody civil war in Castilla (Russell 89). Throughout the period Aragón constantly sought to interfere in Castilla's internal affairs.

The Situation of the Jews

The fourteenth century was a time of crisis for European Jews. Both England and France expelled their small Jewish populations, but Spain did not do so at this time. This may have been because of the prominent positions held by Jews in the administration of the government, at both the royal and the local levels. Jews were also contracted by the king to collect taxes in his name for a commission. The monarchy claimed that the positions of tax collectors were filled by Jews because Christians were not interested in performing this unpopular task (Jackson 105). Jews were employed not only by the government, but also by large landowners, and even by military orders,[1] to handle their economic affairs. They also served as moneylenders, filling the need to provide loans to Christians, who were prohibited from lending money at interest to other Christians. Because Jews held all of these positions, and because they were taxed at a higher rate than Christians, they made a very significant contribution to the tax base.

Although the Jews were not expelled from Spain at this time, and they were not prevented from holding important positions, they were under pressure to convert for various reasons. Dominican and Franciscan friars were pressuring the government to remove Jews from such high positions. Accepting conversion helped the Jews to keep their posts. These Jewish upper classes were also facing censure from Jewish zealots who were attacking them for their liberal attitudes, and conversion was one way of saving them-

---

1. The military orders were monastic orders established for military purposes. In reward for the effectiveness of their service to the monarchy during the Reconquest, the orders were awarded extensive estates. The master of the order held a very high position in the kingdom because he had an army at his command and enjoyed large revenues from the land held by the order. The three most powerful Spanish orders were Santiago, Alcántara, and Calatrava, the Order of Santiago being by far the most powerful. It has been estimated that these three orders commanded more than a million vassals.

selves from this type of criticism (Russell 93). Those who accepted conversion were known as *conversos*.

In 1391, a series of pogroms began in Sevilla and spread north through Castilla and Aragón, decimating Jewish communities. The persecution and massacre of so many Jews forced many to convert. In fact, conversions were so frequent that it was said, "the supply of holy oil ran out" (Russell 93). It would be natural to question the sincerity of their conversion under these circumstances, and apparently that sincerity was seriously questioned, as Fernán Pérez indicates in *Pen Portraits*. Although subsequent monarchs tried to control anti-Semitic activity, the Jews never did regain the situation they had enjoyed in Spain before the pogroms.

Some of the Jews who did not convert were able to keep their positions, but many were replaced by *conversos* and by *cristianos viejos*, a term meaning 'Old Christians' that was used to describe someone who had no Jewish or Moorish blood. The *conversos*, however, continued to be resented by the lower classes as well as by the lesser clergy because of the high positions they held. Because of the antagonism shown against them, Jews favored a strong monarchy, which they felt would provide them with protection.

The Ascent of the Trastámara Line and the Expansion of the Nobility

In 1350, King Alfonso XI died, leaving his son Pedro as official heir. Pedro I, later dubbed "the Cruel" by his detractors, was Alfonso's son by his Portuguese wife, María. However, Alfonso also left twin sons by his mistress, Leonor de Guzmán: Enrique, Count of Trastámara; and Fadrique, Master of Santiago. Enrique's attempts to wrest the throne from his half-brother Pedro sparked a civil war that lasted the length of Pedro's reign.

Pedro represented a force for centralization, a strong monarchy following the law code of Alfonso X. A group of nobles and the small Castilian bourgeoisie favored this concept and became Pedro's followers. England, Portugal, and Navarra also supported Pedro's claim to the throne. England's support was due, in part, to the fact that Pedro's daughter, Constance, was married to John of Gaunt, who was the fourth son of the English King Edward III.

Pedro's half-brother Enrique of Trastámara, who favored the decentralizing Germanic tradition of governing, had the support of the Pope, the French, and the Aragonese. Within Castilla, the nobility who supported that same tradition also became his followers. Because of the underlying support of England and France for Pedro and Enrique respectively, Spain became embroiled in the Hundred Years War.

The civil war went on until 1369. It ended when Enrique of Trastámara assassinated Pedro and then seized the throne, becoming Enrique II (1369–79). In order to repay his debt to those who had supported him, and to gain further support for the Trastámara line, Enrique gave to his followers large gifts of royal land, which were called *mercedes*, and he also bestowed upon them the feudal titles of duke, marquis, and count. This practice was continued by his son, Juan I (1379–90), and created a whole new class of Castilian nobility unrelated by blood to the monarchy. Thus, a new group of nobles with significant land holdings was added to the existing noble class, who already had huge tracts of land acquired during the Reconquest.[2] During the thirteenth century, lands that had been recaptured from the Moors were given to select noble families, to the clergy, and to the military orders of Santiago, Calatrava, and Alcántara. Those who received these lands established large estates called *señoríos*, which surrounded royal property. *Pen Portraits* includes descriptions of several members of the noble families that controlled these estates: the Velascos, the Manriques, the Stúñigas, the Mendozas, the Enríquez, and others.

2. The Reconquest (718–1492) refers to the time period in Iberian history in which Christians were attempting to recapture lands previously taken from them by the Moors (Moslem invaders who entered Spain from northern Africa in 711). By the mid fifteenth century, Castilla was clearly the dominant force in this effort, and the only remaining stronghold of the Moors was the Kingdom of Granada.

These practices led to an increasingly powerful land-holding class. Castilla's economy remained essentially dependent on the land for maintaining self-sufficiency in food production and for sheep grazing to support her flourishing wool trade. The revenues derived from that trade were so substantial that there was no incentive to develop manufacturing capabilities. Therefore, urban development was limited to port and market towns, and no effective urban middle class arose to balance the social and economic power of the landholders. The nobility depended on the land for the production of their wealth. They controlled the lands that they held, and the villages located on those lands. They not only benefited from the flocks that they owned, but also collected taxes on the flocks that either grazed on or passed through their lands.

This increase in the size and wealth of the noble class fueled the already existing conflict between two general factions, one broadly supporting a strong monarchy, the other, seeking to limit the monarch's power by giving the aristocracy a stronger voice in the governing of the Kingdom. At the same time, although the towns were attempting to maintain their rights against incursions by both the monarchy and the great landowners, they often viewed the growth of the monarch's power as a counterbalance to the power of the landed magnates.

The Reign of Juan I

In 1379, Juan I succeeded his father, Enrique II, and confirmed the *mercedes* that his father had granted. During his reign, Juan had conflicts with both the English and their allies, the Portuguese. Juan had married the heiress to the Portuguese throne, Beatriz. After the death of Beatriz's father, King Fernando, Juan attacked Portugal and attempted to take the throne. However, he and his French allies were defeated at Aljubarrota in 1385.

During Juan I's reign, England invaded Castilla twice (1381, 1387). England, looking to remove the pro-French Tratámaras from power, supported the return to the throne of Pedro's descendants, since Pedro's daughter Constance was married to John of Gaunt. However, the Castilians finally defeated the English, and the claim was put to rest when Catalina, the daughter of John of Gaunt and Constance, married Juan I's son, the future Enrique III.

The Reign of Enrique III

Enrique III (1390–1406), whose portrait is the first in Fernán Pérez's collection, succeeded his father, Juan I, when he was eleven years old. The three years of his minority were marked by turbulence. Three groups vied for power in the governing of the Kingdom: those who defended a powerful monarchy, those nobles looking to increase their authority, and town representatives seeking greater voice in government. Also, an outbreak of anti-Semitism led to the devastating pogroms of 1391.

Enrique was declared king in 1393 and managed to reclaim some of the *mercedes* and subsidies that had been granted during his minority. His reign was generally peaceful. Castilla was still allied with the French, but because of Enrique's marriage to Catalina, Castilla enjoyed better relations with England. There was conflict with the Moors, who had attacked Christian holdings. Enrique's forces enjoyed some victories against the Moors, and Enrique would have pursued the war effort against them had he not died in 1406.

The Minority of Juan II

The reign of Enrique III's son, Juan II (1406–54), began, as his father's had, with a regency. Fernán Pérez tells us that Enrique III left clear instructions in his will for the care of his son. Juan's custody and upbringing was put in the hands of Diego López de Stúñiga and Juan de Velasco. However, Juan's mother, Catalina, refused to relinquish her infant son and was awarded his custody. The child's education was entrusted to Pablo de Santa María. In addition to these provisions, the will appointed Queen Catalina and Enrique III's brother, Fernando, as co-regents. Fernán Pérez provides a portrait of each of these individuals and presents all of them in a favorable light, but he seems to hold none of them in higher esteem than he does Fernando.

There was tension between Catalina and Fernando during the regency, but eventually Fernando became dominant and proved to be an able regent, promoting internal peace, and peace with England and Portugal. One of his accomplishments as co-regent was the defeat of the Moors at the city of Antequera, for which he became known as Fernando of Antequera. When the King of Aragón, Martín I, died without an heir, Fernando, who was his nephew, had a claim to the throne. In 1412, a commission that convened at Caspe recognized that claim and declared him king. He continued as a regent of Castilla until his death in 1416.

Although he may have restrained his own ambitions in Castilla, Fernando left his descendants with great revenues and in positions of power so that they would have great influence in Castilian politics. Fernando had large land-holdings, stretching from Portugal to Navarra and Aragón, which he left to his descendants. Highfield suggests that Fernando's intention was to leave his descendants as protectors of the monarchy, acting as intermediaries between nobles and monarch. They would be active in the governing of the Kingdom, and one step above the higher nobility (Highfield 124). Others suggest that his intention was to leave his descendants in such a position that nothing could be accomplished in Castilla without their support (de la Cierva 176). Those of his sons who were the most influential in Castilian politics were the following: Alfonso, who succeeded his father as King of Aragón; Juan, who became King of Navarra; Enrique, Master of the Order of Santiago; and Sancho, Master of the Order of Alcántara. Two of Fernando's daughters became queens: Leonor, Queen of Portugal; and María, wife of Juan II and Queen of Castilla.

Fernando's sons had the wherewithal and the desire to interfere in Castilian politics, which they began to do at the end of the regency. His sons Juan and Enrique, referred to as the *Infantes* of Aragón, led parties of nobles who constantly challenged the power of Juan II in Castilla.

The Reign of Juan II

In 1419, Juan II reached fourteen years of age, and the *Cortes*[3] proclaimed him king. His reign was characterized by constant civil war. On one side, defenders of a strong monarchy were led by Juan II's favorite, Álvaro de Luna (1390–1453). Don Álvaro,[4] the illegitimate son of a wealthy Aragonese *converso* family, lived in the royal household and tutored Juan from the age of eight. De Luna's influence over Juan was so great that it was he who really headed the government. On the opposing side were members of the nobility who fought to increase their role in the governing of the Kingdom. They frequently joined forces with the *Infantes* of Aragón, who were seeking to advance their own interests in Castilla. However, this alliance was unstable. When the nobles realized that the *Infantes* represented a threat to their interests, they changed sides and supported Álvaro de Luna. Our author was known to be an opponent of Don Álvaro, yet in the treatment of this man's character, he avoided the practice common among his contemporaries of presenting historical figures as thoroughly good or thoroughly evil persons. Instead, he presented both the virtues and vices of Don Álvaro, and did the same in describing those nobles who opposed de Luna, and whose cause Pérez himself espoused. Speaking

---

3. The *Cortes* was a political assembly presided over by the king, which was originally comprised of representatives of the clergy, the nobility, and the towns. By the time of Juan II, the clergy and the nobility had lost interest in the *Cortes*, and only representatives of the towns attended sessions with any degree of regularity. Many of these men were appointed by the king and paid by him to attend, so it can in no sense be considered a democratic assembly.

4. *Don* is a title of respect used only with a man's first name.

of these nobles, he declared, "The greed of the great knights is not to be pardoned. These knights, in order to augment their estates and incomes, set aside their consciences and their love for their country." (100)

Juan II's reign may be divided into four stages according to political events: Álvaro de Luna slowly rises to power (1419–30); differences between Álvaro de Luna and the nobles become apparent (1430–37); nobles rebel against de Luna (1437–45); Don Álvaro loses his power and his life (1445–53) (de la Cierva 180).

As soon as Juan II was declared king in 1419, the *Infantes* of Aragón, Prince Juan and Prince Enrique, began to seek control of the young monarch. Prince Juan tried to increase his power on the King's advisory council by appointing to it nobles who supported him. It was his plan that this Royal Council, with him at its head, would then govern the Kingdom. If Prince Juan and Prince Enrique had remained united, there would have been no one strong enough to oppose them. However, differences arose between the two brothers very quickly, and Prince Enrique, Master of Santiago, found support among another group of nobles. In 1420, while Prince Juan was in Navarra, Enrique, taking advantage of his brother's absence, took control of the young King at the royal residence in Tordesillas, and took over the governing of the Kingdom. Prince Juan reacted by leading his troops against his brother. It was Álvaro de Luna who arranged the escape of Juan II on November 29, 1420. They sought refuge in the deserted castle of Montalbán. Although Enrique surrounded the castle, he was reluctant to attack, and he abandoned the site as his brother Juan and his troops approached.

The result of this action left Prince Juan and Álvaro de Luna in power. Prince Enrique and one of his supporters, Garci Fernández Manrique, were imprisoned. Other followers, Ruy López Dávalos and Pedro Manrique, escaped prison by fleeing. Álvaro de Luna had the support of a group of nobles who were convinced that only an increase in the power of the monarchy would bring stability. A new Royal Council was created, including Álvaro de Luna, Prince Juan, and the following nobles: Count Fadrique; the Archbishop of Toledo; Admiral Alfonso Enríquez; Chief Justice Pedro de Stúñiga; Governor Diego Gómez de Sandoval; the Count of Benavente Rodrigo Alfonso Pimentel; and Fernán Alfonso de Robles. Of the many nobles who are part of this history and whose portraits appear in this text, Alfonso de Robles has the singular distinction of having been described by Fernán Pérez as the very embodiment of all that was wrong with Castilla at that moment in history.

During this time period, the influence of the *Cortes* was reduced. In 1422, the *Cortes* met at Ocaña and decided that town representatives would be paid by the king and not by the cities they represented. This strengthened the monarch's power over the *Cortes*. Besides the monarch, a large number of nobles benefited from the defeat of Prince Enrique. Possessions of the losing side were liberally distributed to supporters of Don Álvaro and Prince Juan, creating a group of grateful partisans.

Don Álvaro, however, was the one who benefited most. He became Constable, and, as such, was the commander of the royal army. His goals now were to eliminate Prince Juan from power and to keep peace with other kingdoms so that he would not have more than one enemy to deal with at a time. He established good relations with England, France, and Portugal, and signed a truce with Granada.

Don Álvaro's plans were challenged when Alfonso V, King of Aragón, decided to make peace between his two brothers, Juan and Enrique. He sought to gain Prince Enrique's freedom, recover Enrique's seized lands, and break the alliance between Prince Juan and Don Álvaro. Thus, the power would be left in the hands of the Aragonese. Although Alfonso V had been in Italy pursuing Aragonese interests there, he returned to Aragón and, by threat of force, succeeded in obtaining Enrique's release and reconciling his two brothers. The Aragonese were now united. Prince Juan, now King of Navarra through his marriage, became the leader of the Aragonese faction and of their supporters in Castilla. Don Álvaro was exiled (1427).

Through all of these changes in leaders, Juan II always remained official King of Castilla, but at this point, King Juan of Navarra was the effective ruler of the country. Redistribution of property and rents continued. The new government failed to provide stability. By 1428, the Castilian nobility, unhappy with the authoritarianism of Juan of Navarra and fearing an outright takeover by Aragón, brought Don Álvaro back. King Juan of Navarra and Prince Enrique lacked the support of their brother Alfonso V, who had returned to his war in Italy. Left to their own resources, they were unable to defeat the forces of Don Álvaro. They were forced to sign a treaty at Majano in 1430, and they left Castilla. The Treaty of Majano effectively established a government by an oligarchy led by Don Álvaro. Other principal figures included Governor Pedro Manrique, Admiral Enríquez, and the Count of Benavente.

At this point, Don Álvaro was at the height of his power and wealth. In addition to being Constable, he became Master of Santiago. He arranged his second marriage with Juana Pimentel, daughter of the Count of Benavente and niece of both Pedro Manrique and Admiral Enríquez. This union cemented his relationship with these nobles. Like Fernando of Antequera before him, Don Álvaro concentrated large possessions under his control. In addition to the lands he acquired when he became Master of Santiago, he further increased his landholdings when he imprisoned the mother of Juan and Enrique.

Under his leadership, a period of seven years of relative peace ensued. Castilla continued at peace with Portugal, maintained good relations with the Pope, and confirmed its alliance with France. In 1430, Castilla signed a treaty with England guaranteeing free trade, and its trading position with other European countries also improved. At home Don Álvaro renewed the campaign against the Moors in Granada, over whom he enjoyed an important victory at La Higueruela.

Within the Kingdom, Don Álvaro responded to threats against him by imprisoning his enemies. He arbitrarily persecuted individuals who held positions that he might want to pass on to one of his relatives. For example, taking advantage of a dispute between the Archbishop of Sevilla, Diego de Anaya, and some members of Anaya's religious order, Don Álvaro removed the Archbishop from his post. He then gave the position to his brother, Juan de Cerezuela. Eventually, Don Álvaro made his brother Archbishop of Toledo, but Anaya never regained his former position.

Although relative peace reigned in the Kingdom, town representatives to the *Cortes* protested the growing power of the grandees and their own loss of the right to name judicial officials. They were powerless, however, to demand any changes. Unfavorable economic conditions and an unjust judicial system provoked unrest among the peasants, and many of them sought the protection afforded by living on the lands of one of the magnates.

Also discontent with their situation, Juan and Enrique, the *Infantes* of Aragón, returned to the Kingdom to occupy properties that they had inherited from their father. They attempted to lead a revolt against Don Álvaro, and they depended upon the support of those Castilian nobles who resented Don Álvaro's power. The uprising failed, leaving Don Álvaro in a position to dictate a reconciliation with Juan and Enrique.

In 1436, Don Álvaro and the *Infantes* came to the following agreement: Juan and Enrique were to leave Castilla and were not to return without the permission of Juan II; Juan II agreed to pay the dowry of his sister Catalina, who was married to Enrique; Juan II promised to marry his son and heir, Enrique, to Juan's daughter; Juan II agreed that the two brothers would receive the annual rents to which they were entitled.

The *Infantes'* resistance now under control, members of the powerful Castilian noble class who had once supported Don Álvaro feared that there was nothing in the way of his power. They became intent upon thwarting his efforts to increase royal authority. Now the conflict was between the Castilian nobles and Don Álvaro. It erupted in outright rebellion in 1437, but since neither side was able to defeat the other, both factions appealed to the *Infantes* for support. Because Don Álvaro represented the monarchy against rebellious nobility, he hoped to receive the sympathy and support of Juan, who, himself, was a monarch. The *Infantes*, however, decided to divide their support between the two sides: Juan sided with Don Álvaro, and Enrique, with the nobles. The power of the two factions now in balance, the *Infantes* were in a position to be arbiters. Don Álvaro retreated to Medina del Campo and was eventually exiled. Although he tried to resist, he was defeated in 1441.

Prince Enrique led the nobles, whose aim it was to set up the Royal Council as the governing body, somewhat independent of the King. They presented their demands to the King, proposing a contractual regime in which the Kingdom's liberties and rights would be assured by the executive body, the Council; the representative body, the *Cortes;* and the judicial body, called the *Audiencia,* which was the supreme organ of civil justice. The Council would be in charge of granting *mercedes,* making treaties, and naming judicial officials to the towns. The *Cortes* would deliberate and present petitions to the King. The *Audiencia* would be the body responsible for judicial decisions. The plan represented rule by the nobility rather than by the central authority of the King.

Although the plan sounded like a change, the result was merely the replacement of one faction with another, putting the Aragonese in control. The Council was dominated by the Aragonese faction, and the *Cortes* still had no real power. Nobles continued to skirmish with each other, attempting to increase their holdings, sometimes at the expense of the cities. There were battles against the forces of Don Álvaro, who still had the support of the King.

In 1443, Prince Juan attempted to solidify his position by expelling all supporters of Don Álvaro. In a coup, he took control of Juan II at Rámaga, and made him a virtual prisoner, an act that infuriated the Castilian nobility, who had not intended to replace one authoritarian figure with another. The nobles again turned to Don Álvaro. And Don Álvaro, with the support of the Castilian Crown Prince Enrique, found himself at the head of the Castilian army. At the Battle of Olmedo, May 19, 1445, the forces under Don Álvaro soundly defeated the troops of Juan and Enrique. Enrique died from complications of a wound to the thigh, which he suffered in that battle, and Juan returned to his Kingdom, Navarra, never to return to Castilla.

Although the victory at Olmedo seemed to cement the position and power of Don Álvaro, he was not the clear victor. Castilan Crown Prince Enrique took credit for the victory and benefited from the spoils. He granted amnesty to the losers, thereby gaining supporters.

Thus, the decisive defeat of the *Infantes* did not result in political stability, since there were still two political factions contesting control of the Kingdom. One consisted of nobles supporting Crown Prince Enrique and his powerful favorite, Juan Pacheco, Marquis of Villena; the other was made up of Don Álvaro, still the favorite of the King, and his supporters. Don Álvaro, despite the amnesty declared by Prince Enrique, divided up holdings of the defeated nobles. This almost led to armed conflict between the two sides, but negotiations resulted in a compromise between Crown Prince Enrique and Don Álvaro. Don Álvaro and Juan Pacheco would act as equals in the service of the King and in the execution of justice.

Don Álvaro depended on Portugal to support his position. He attempted to fortify this support by arranging a marriage between the widowed Juan II and Isabel, granddaughter of King Juan I of

Portugal. Don Álvaro used his influence over Juan II to achieve this union, although Juan himself would have preferred a French alliance. However, the new Queen turned out to be one of Don Álvaro's most dangerous enemies.

Castilla's internal instability was reflected in armed conflict, both at its borders and within its boundaries. There were battles on the front with Granada, in which the Moors took back several positions that the Christians had previously reconquered. Don Álvaro attacked holdings of Juan, King of Navarra. There were unproductive skirmishes with Aragón. Within the Kingdom, there was constant conflict among the members of the lesser nobility. In the summer of 1447 it seemed that "the whole Kingdom of Castilla was in flames" (Suárez Fernández 397).

On May 1, 1448, Don Álvaro, taking advantage of his reconciliation with the Crown Prince, took over the government in a coup at Záfraga. He imprisoned important members of the nobility, including the Counts of Alba and Benavente, Enrique Enríquez, and Pedro and Suero de Quiñones. Other nobles escaped imprisonment by fleeing. Don Álvaro sought support from his Portuguese allies, but they were not in a position to aid him. Those nobles who had fled received economic support from the Aragonese and took control of Murcia. Other sites in Castilla, including Toledo and the lands of the Count of Benavente, rebelled.

Don Álvaro's position looked hopeless, but his fortune seemed to change when Murcia began to negotiate for peace, the lands of Benavente surrendered, and an Aragonese invasion was repelled. Although Don Álvaro again appeared to be in control, other problems arose. He had plans to take Béjar, the stronghold of Pedro de Stúñiga, leader of the faction of nobles who opposed Don Álvaro's usurpation of power. Alonso Pérez de Vivero, a trusted follower whom Don Álvaro had raised up from the lower nobility, however, betrayed those plans. Furthermore, Don Álvaro had somehow lost the affection of King Juan II, at least partly due to

Queen Isabel's enmity toward him. The Queen forwarded a message from Juan II to the nobles, stating that the King wanted to be freed from Álvaro de Luna's influence. Don Álvaro exacerbated the situation by killing Pérez de Vivero on April 1, 1453. On April 3, the King ordered Don Álvaro's imprisonment. Although Don Álvaro had the opportunity to flee, he did not. He accepted his fate stoically, and seemed to prefer death to any less honorable solution. A witness stated that when Don Álvaro was brought before the King, he told him that he was a man who knew how to die. He said that he was under the King's power, and, therefore, the King should do with him what he pleased (Suárez Fernández 402).

Juan II appointed a commission to determine if the death penalty against Don Álvaro was justified. The commission agreed to the sentence, but said that the order would have to be signed by the King himself. Don Álvaro was beheaded in Valladolid on June 3, 1453. The King also died in Valladolid thirteen months later, on July 21, 1454. He was reported to have said that he wished he had been born the son of a peasant and that he had become a monk and not the King of Castilla (Suárez Fernández 403).

Fernán Pérez de Guzmán: The Author and His Works

Fernán Pérez de Guzmán was born c. 1377, son of Pedro Suárez de Toledo and Elvira de Ayala. He was an historian, moralist, politician, and poet who was an important link in a family chain of famous figures. He was nephew of Chancellor Pedro de Ayala, uncle of the Marqués de Santillana, and great grandfather of Garcilaso de la Vega.[5] He died c. 1460.

---

5. Pedro López de Ayala (1332–1407) was one of the most significant literary figures of his day. He was court chronicler to four kings: Pedro I (the Cruel), Enrique II, Juan I, and Enrique III. He was also a poet and a prolific translator. His major poetic work, *Rimado del Palacio (Palace Verses)* is a courtier's autobiography that satirizes life

We know very little about his early life, but we do know that he spent almost thirty of his final years in relative seclusion at his estate in Batres, having retired there sometime in 1432. Whether his exile was self-imposed because of his disillusionment with the social and political state of Castilla, or whether he had been forced into exile for political reasons is not certain.

Although Fernán Pérez dedicated himself to study and to writing in Batres, he did not completely disassociate himself from the company of such erudite visitors to his estate as his cousin Vasco de Guzmán, Archdeacon of Toledo; Alvar García de Santa María, presumed author of a large portion of the *Crónica de don Juan II* [Chronicle of Juan II]; Alfonso de Cartagena, author of *Rerum Hispanorum*; and Gonzalo de Ocaña, prior of the convent of Santa María de Sisla, Order of St. Jerome. It was during this time that he wrote his major work of history entitled *Mar de Historias* [Sea of Histories], of which the present text is a part. The *Mar de Historias* was composed of three books: the first, a collection of brief biographies of emperors and princes; the second, on the lives and works of the saints; and the third, the present volume, on illustrious Castilians. The first two books were based on the *Mare Historiarum* of Giovanni de Colonna. The third book, the author himself tells us, was modeled after the *Historia Troiana* of Guido delle Colonne.[6]

---

in the palace. Among his translations are the works of Livy, Boethius, St. Gregory the Great, St. Isidore, and Boccaccio.

The Marques de Santillana, Iñigo López de Mendoza (1398–1458), was a soldier, a statesman, and one of the most widely read poets of fifteenth-century Spain. He was greatly influenced by Dante, Petrarch, and other Italian poets, and was the first to write sonnets in Spanish.

Garcilaso de la Vega (c. 1501–36), the most representative lyricist of the Spanish Golden Age, is frequently referred to as the perfect Renaissance gentleman, in the style of Castiglione's *Cortegiano* [Book of the courtier], a work which he greatly admired and which he convinced his compatriot Boscón to translate into Spanish. Most memorable among his works are his eclogues and sonnets in which he introduced Italian metrical forms into his verse.

6. Many suggest—and we agree—that the format and style of *Pen Portraits* more closely resembles that of *Mare Historiarum* in that both are collections of individual

Although Fernán Pérez is best remembered for his prose, and specifically for the present text, his poetic output was considerable and perhaps underrated. His most often mentioned poetic work is *Loores de los claros varones de Castilla* [In praise of the illustrious men of Castilla], an historic poem that lauds the unsung valor and virtue of the principal figures of Spanish history. According to our author, the glory of these forgotten men would have been known and perpetuated if only Spain had been blessed, as Greece had been, with the good fortune of having someone such as Homer to recount their deeds.

His other poetic works include *Coronaciones de las cuatro virtudes* [Coronation of the four virtues], an allegory dedicated to his nephew, the Marqués de Santillana; *Los Proverbios* [Proverbs], a collection of religious and moral proverbs; *Coplas de vicios e virtudes* [Verses of vice and virtue]; *Floresta de los Philósophos* [Collection of maxims of the philosophers], a series of maxims taken from the works of Seneca, Cicero, St. Bernard, and others; and several poems that have appeared in other collected works, such as in the *Cancionero de Baena* [The songbook of Baena].

About This Work

Pen Portraits of Illustrious Castilians [*Generaciones y Semblanzas*] is a compilation of thirty-four biographical sketches of the most illustrious Castilians of the mid fifteenth century. These include three kings, a queen, and thirty nobles, prelates, and scholars who represent the most prominent families of the day: the Trastámaras, the Manriques, the Mendozas, the Enriques, the Stúñigas, the Quiñones, and others.

---

biographies that describe the lineage and principal characteristics of their subjects. We believe that Fernán Pérez is saying here that his work is modeled after Guido's in the sense that his expressed objective, like Guido's, is to immortalize great men who were valiant on the battlefield and wise and honorable in the governing of their people.

In each sketch, Pérez de Guzmán first outlines the family background of his subject; he then lists his or her physical characteristics, personality traits, remarkable deeds, virtues, and vices. Fernán Pérez was among the first to depart from the practice of presenting an historical figure as a perfect example of vice or virtue. Rather, he shows that his characters are mixtures of good and bad. Each sketch ends with information about the time, place, and circumstances of the person's death. With few exceptions, all of the portraits are presented according to this formula.

The author gives the impression that any information he has included in his sketches, he has gleaned either through personal contact with the subjects or through the testimony of witnesses. Whenever possible, he corroborates his commentary with written testimony in order to bolster the authenticity of his own writing. He mentions in several places in the work that the amount of written testimony in the annals of Castilian history is very scarce because of the lamentable destruction of historical documents and the almost total disregard for preserving the past that has prevailed throughout Castilian history.[7]

Occasionally the author digresses within one of the portraits to comment on other topics, such as the inscrutable workings of Divine Providence, the nature of good and evil, the acceptance of re-

---

7. Fernán Pérez refers here to the political, religious, and moral censure that prevailed during, and prior to, the fifteenth century on the Iberian Peninsula. As early as 587, after the Visigoth King Recaredo had converted to Catholicism, he ordered the burning of all Arian manuscripts. During the Moorish Invasion and the Reconquest, entire libraries in Andalucía were destroyed by both Moors and Christians. During the Middle Ages penalties inflicted upon authors of subversive texts were very severe, a situation that served as a deterrent to prospective writers and caused readers to hide or even destroy any such texts in their possession. Both monarchs and prelates are known to have ordered the burning of private libraries containing volumes that opposed the political or moral stances that they favored, as in the case of the destruction of the library of Enrique de Villena by Bishop Lope de Barrientos acting under the order of Juan II. Also, during the Trastámara depuration of Castilian archives, innumerable literary and historical documents were lost forever (Deyermond, *La literatura perdida* 22–23).

cent converts to Christianity, and the greed and self-serving motives of many of his contemporaries.

The author's prolog to his text has received more commentary from both historians and literary scholars than have the sketches themselves. This introduction appears to be the first treatise written in Spanish on the nature of history and on the duties and responsibilities of those who undertake recording it. Deyermond praises the novelty of the prolog when he writes that "Fernán Pérez does for history what Santillana had done for poetry a year or so before" (*A Literary History* 153). Just as Santillana was the first to give a systematic account of the main qualities and defects of the poets he mentions, Fernán Pérez was the first to give a coherent account of how history should be written, listing the requisite qualities and experience of those who attempt to record it. Fernán Pérez insists that for history to be recorded honestly and accurately, it should be written only by those who themselves have witnessed the events they describe, or who have received information from eyewitnesses known to be reliable and unbiased. Furthermore, he requires that no history be published until after the death of those whose deeds are being recorded. This is to insure that no king, prince, or powerful noble might influence the historian's writing. The historian's responsibility, he maintains, is to accurately and objectively record the actions of mankind for posterity, but he has a responsibility of equal importance to those who actually participated in the making of history. Those who through valor and self-sacrifice accomplished great deeds deserve the fame and glory that the historian has the power, and the obligation, to preserve for them. Although Fernán Pérez clearly states that this work is not a history, but rather a "registry or memorial" to the two kings who reigned during his lifetime, he does abide by the guidelines that he has set down for historians. In fact, the first version of his work, published in 1450, consisted of only 32 portraits; the sketches of Juan II and Álvaro de Luna were not added until 1455, after they had died.

Another innovative feature of this work is that it is the first collection of biographies in Spanish historiography. Prior to, and during, Fernán Pérez's time, there were several single-subject biographies written. The *Crónica de Pedro Niño* [The chronicle of Pedro Niño], on the life of the Count of Buelna, appeared in 1448. The Count was patron of his biographer, Gutierre de Games. Another biography was the *Relación de los hechos del condestable Miguel Lucas de Irazco* [An account of the deeds of the constable Miguel Lucas de Irazco], an anonymous text that chronicles the Constable's life between 1458 and 1471. The fifteenth century also saw a continued flourishing of chronicles of individual reigns, which might also be included in the category of single-subject biographies. Notable among these are the works of Pedro López de Ayala, court chronicler to four kings and uncle of Fernán Pérez. The one outstanding autobiography of the period is the memoirs of Leonor López de Córdoba, a moving account of the imprisonment and suffering of her family during the reign of Enrique III because of their political affiliation with Pedro I. Although the work describes events that occurred between 1369 and 1380, the text was not completed until 1410.

After *Pen Portraits*, it was a full generation before another collection of biographical sketches appeared in Spanish history. In 1486, Fernando del Pulgar completed his *Claros Varones de Castilla* [Illustrious men of Castilla], a work strongly influenced by Fernán Pérez's text. *Claros Varones* has as its cast of characters the next generation of Castilian nobility and clerics.

Manuscript Tradition of *Generaciones y Semblanzas*

The oldest known manuscript of *Generaciones y Semblanzas* is from the fifteenth century and is housed in the Biblioteca Escorial in Spain, Codex Z-III-2, folios 91–120. There are three other manuscripts of the text: two in the Biblioteca Nacional in Madrid; the other in the British Museum in London.

The first of the two in the Biblioteca Nacional, MS 6156, contains an historical miscellany from the sixteenth century. The *Generaciones*, which lacks its first seven folios, comprises folios 57–73. The manuscript was purchased in 1757 from Antonio López de Zúñiga, Count of Miranda.

The second manuscript in the same library, MS 1619, is an historical miscellany from the seventeenth century. The first twenty-four folios contain *Generaciones* along with a dedication to Luisa de Padilla, Countess of Aranda, by Pedro de Rozas, a professed monk of the Order of St. Jerome, Monastery of Fresdelval.

The manuscript of the British Museum, Egerton 310, is also a mix of seventeenth-century historical texts. In addition to the *Generaciones*, folios 277–311, this manuscript contains the *Crónica de Enrique IV* [Chronicle of Enrique IV], which is attributed to Alonso de Palencia and a prologue to that chronicle by Diego Enríquez del Castillo. The manuscript was purchased from Obadiah Rich in 1835. This version of the *Generaciones* appears to be related to the MS 1619 because they bear similar chapter titles (Tate xxii).

The first printed edition of *Generaciones*, which includes the rest of *Mar de Historias* in the same codex, was printed in Valladolid in 1512 by Diego Gumiel. The text reinforces the authority of the Escorial manuscript but appears not to be a copy of it. (Bordona xxxi). It is preceded by a dedication to Martín de Angulo, Bishop of Córdoba, and was edited by Cristóbal de Santisteban. Santisteban, who was known for the liberties he frequently took in modifying, amplifying, or suppressing entire sentences of a text, omitted in the case of *Generaciones* the entire portrait of Sancho de Rojas (Bordona xxviii).

A second edition was undertaken in Logroño in 1517 and includes the *Crónica de Juan II* [Chronicle of Juan II]. The editor, Galíndez de Carvajal, who had rewritten several other historical texts, further modified *Generaciones*, even to the point of including reference to persons who lived, and events that occurred, after the death of the author. The Galíndez edition, which appears to be related to MS 6156, became the source of several future printed editions: Sevilla, 1543; Pamplona, 1590; Pamplona, 1591; Madrid, 1678; Madrid, 1775; Valencia, 1779; Madrid, 1790; Madrid, 1877. Bordona tells us that shortly after the publication of the 1775 edition, Llaguno, its editor, gained access to the Escorial manuscript, which confirmed his fears that the Galíndez text might contain serious modifications to earlier manuscripts. Because his discovery arrived as late as it did, Llaguno's only recourse was to append the omitted portrait of Sancho de Rojas and a list of the principal variants. As surprising as it seems, the three editions that appeared after Llaguno's did not utilize the Escorial manuscript. In fact, almost 150 years passed before an editor, Domínguez Bordona, prepared an edition (Madrid, 1924) based upon this oldest known manuscript.

In 1965 Brian Tate prepared an edition that also utilized the Escorial manuscript. In addition, Tate consulted the MS 1619, the Santisteban printed edition (1512), and the Egerton 310 manuscript. He also had at hand a copy of the *Crónica del Halconero* [Chronicle of the falconer], the introduction of which is a version of Fernán Pérez's prolog to the *Generaciones*.

Translators' Note

In translating this text we have attempted to be as faithful as possible to the original while aiming, above all, at readability. We have tried to extract the author's exact meaning, and then to express it clearly and accurately, adhering as closely to the original syntax and vocabulary as the English language would allow. Translating the title has presented a particularly difficult challenge in this regard. A formal translation would have resulted in *Generations and Biographical Sketches* or *Generations and Portraits*. But, in the context of this work, the Spanish "generación" refers more to familial descent than to the broader concept of "a group of unrelated people born about the same time," as the English "generation" suggests. The meaning we extracted from the title, therefore, was "Portraits (of certain individuals) and the families (of those individuals)". When we decided upon *Pen Portraits of Illustrious Castilians* we were aware that we were taking greater liberty than we had taken at any other point in this translation, but we believe that the English title precisely and clearly expresses the content of the text, and the spirit, if not the form, of the original title.

In the text itself, we have chosen not to eliminate certain stylistic features of fifteenth-century Spanish despite the fact that they are no longer in vogue either in modern Spanish or in English. Among these are the frequent use of "and" in sentence initial position and the ubiquitous pairing of synonymous, or nearly synonymous, adjectives or adverbs, as in "bizarre and extraordinary," "peaceful and tranquil," and "in vain and for naught." We have preserved these features, believing that, even in translation, they reflect the linguistic flavor of a past era. It is for the reader to decide if our decision was a wise one.

In addition to utilizing Brian Tate's critical edition of *Generaciones y Semblanzas*, we have also consulted Domínguez Bordona's earlier edition, which was first published in 1924. We have borrowed many of the footnotes from both editions; they appear as abridged translations of the originals and are credited to the respective editors. All other notes are our own. The notes included are intended to provide quick access to information that might be unfamiliar to the reader. They are meant to serve as a reading aid and make no claim to original research. The English translations of all text titles in both the body of the translation and the footnotes are our own.

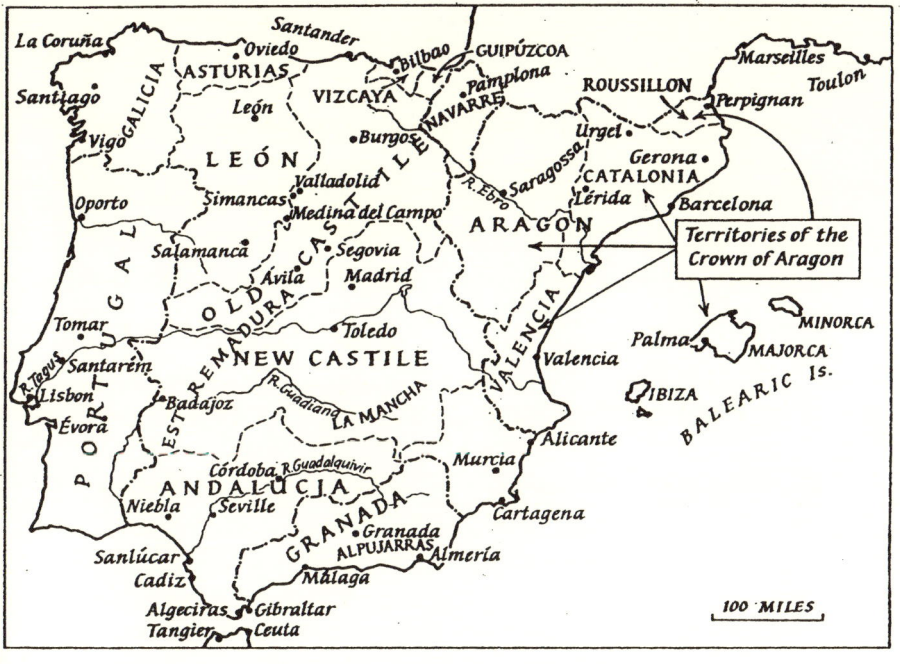

The Territorial Divisions of the Iberian Peninsula at the End of the Middle Ages. This map and the genealogical table on the next page are both reproduced from P.E. Russell's Spain: A Companion to Spanish Studies (1973) with permission from Routledge.

KINGS OF CASTILE AND LEÓN

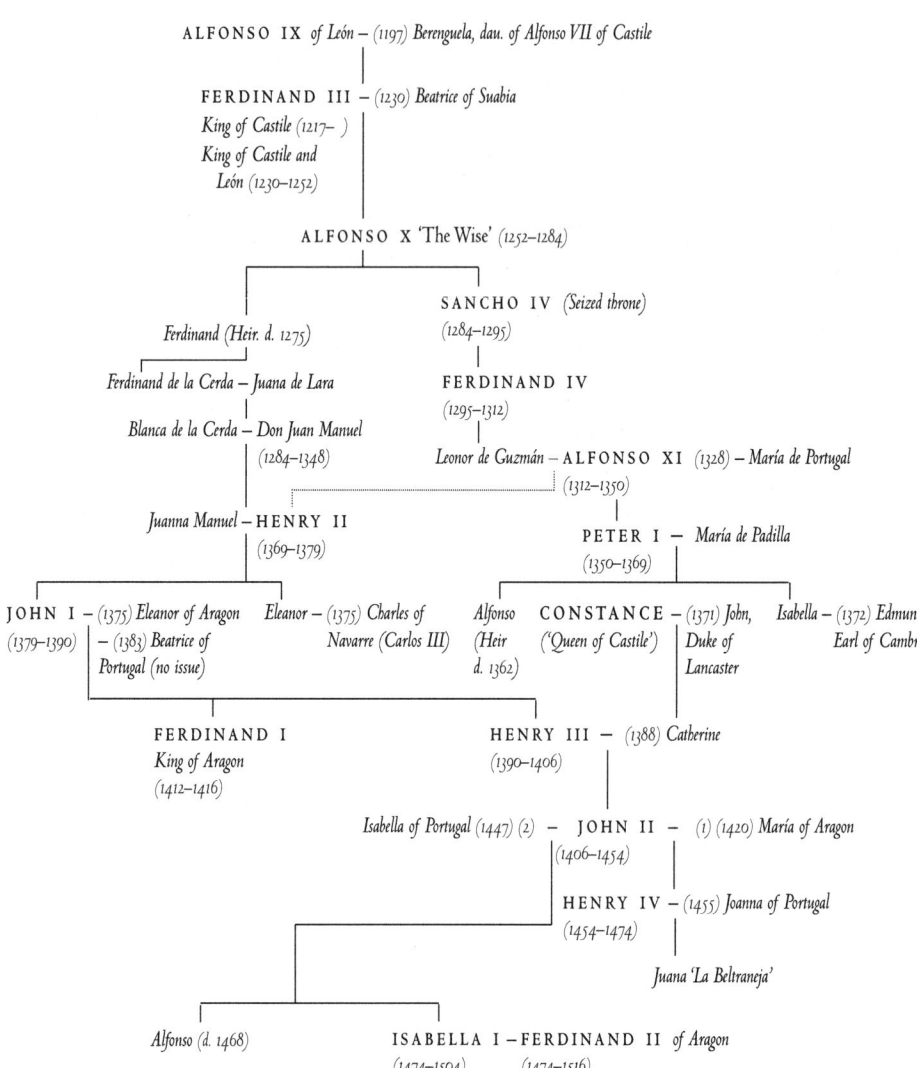

PEN PORTRAITS
OF ILLUSTRIOUS
CASTILIANS

Author's Prolog

The following is a description of the excellent kings of Spain, Don Enrique III and Don Juan II, and of their families, their characteristics, their deeds, and of the venerable prelates and notable knights of their times

Often it happens that the chronicles and histories that tell of powerful kings, notable princes, and great cities are regarded with suspicion and doubt. Little faith is put in their veracity for two particular reasons, among others. First, because some of those who undertake the writing and commentary of ancient matters are shameless men who would rather relate what is bizarre and extraordinary than what is true and exact, in the belief that their story will be regarded as inconsequential if they do not tell of things that are bigger-than-life, even if those things are more worthy of awe than of credulity. One such writer—not of our times—is an insignificant and presumptuous man named Pedro de Corral, who wrote a work called Saracen Chronicle.[1] Others called it the Chronicle of King Rodrigo, but it might more aptly have been entitled "Hogwash" or "Pure Unadulterated Lies." If at the present time we practiced censorship in Castilla—that very important and useful custom practiced in ancient times by the Romans that provided the power to examine and correct the actions of Roman citizens—Pedro de Corral would be deserving of harsh punishment indeed. For surely if an accountant who falsified the books by a small sum of money is deserving of serious punishment, how much more guilty is the chronicler of the notable and memorable deeds of history

---

1. Pedro de Corral wrote the *Crónica del rey don Rodrgo* [Chronicle of King Don Rodrigo] c. 1400, but it was not printed until 1499. Tate

who gives fame and renown to those who do not deserve it, and takes it away from those who, with great danger to their person and great expense to their household, in defense of their religion, and in service to their king, and for the good of their republic and for the honor of their family, accomplished deeds so worthy of mention? What many of these men did, they did more to maintain the glorious and unblemished reputation of their names in the annals of history than to achieve some practical advantage that might come on the heels of such deeds, no matter how great those advantages might be. Anyone who reads Roman history will find that it is so: that there were many Roman princes who asked no recompense or reward for their worthy deeds except recognition or the title of the province that they had defeated or conquered, as in the cases of such men as the three Scipios and the two Metelluses and many others.[2]

Well, if men such as these wanted only that their good reputation be committed to writing and preserved in literature, and if that literature is false, of what advantage to these noble and valiant men is all their work if they are left empty, frustrated, and deprived of their wish and the fruits of their merit, that is, fame!

In my opinion, for history to be written well and accurately, three things are necessary. First, the historian must be wise and discreet and use good rhetoric to tell the story in a pleasing way and in a worthy style, because good form brings honor and beauty to the material.

2. We believe Pérez's mention of three Scipios and two Metelluses was intended to be two Scipios and three Metelluses and refers to the following: Metellus Macedonicus was the Roman general who deposed Andriscus and thus made Macedonia a Roman province. Metellus Numidicus was named for his defeat of the Numidian leader Jugurtha. Metellus Creticus was the consul who, in 69 B.C., commanded the Roman armies that conquered Crete. Scipio Africanus, the Elder, was the Roman general whose victory over the Carthaginians in the Battle of Zoma ended the Second Punic War (202 B.C.). Scipio Africanus, the Younger, was named for his exploits in the Third Punic War (149–146 B.C.). His name Africanus was given in honor of his defeat of Carthage.

Second, the historian should be present at the important events of war and peace. But, since it would be impossible for him to be present in all cases, at least he should have the good judgment to accept information only from those who are trustworthy and who themselves were present at those events. And if this rule is followed without exception, the historian will be able to avail himself of information provided by witnesses. After all, there never was, nor will there ever be, an event of such great magnificence and sanctity as the birth, the life, the Passion, and the Resurrection of our Savior Jesus Christ, yet of his four historians, two were not present at the time, but they wrote what was related to them by others.

The third necessity is that history should not be written while the king or prince whose era or reign is being recorded is still alive, so that the historian can be free to write the truth without fear.

And so, precisely because these rules are not followed, chronicles are suspect and lacking in truth, which does no small harm. Since a good reputation in this world is the true recompense and reward of those who work so diligently to attain it, if that reputation is distorted and falsely represented in history, those magnificent kings and princes have truly worked in vain and for naught when they went to war and made conquests, and when they were just and generous and merciful, which perhaps makes them even more notable and worthy of fame and glory than do their victories in battle and conquest.

The same is true of the valiant and virtuous knights who devote themselves to practicing loyalty to their king and to defending their country and the bond of their friendships, and who do so without questioning the cost or fearing death.

The same is true of the great learned men and scholars who carefully and diligently compile and edit books to fight against heresy as well as to increase the faith and devotion of Christians, to exercise justice, and to impart moral doctrine. And for all of their efforts in doing such virtuous work and in accomplishing deeds so useful to the Republic, how are these men rewarded if their reputation is denied them and attributed to negligent and vile men at the whimsy of the—I cannot say "historians"—I must say "prevaricators"?

Certainly, a great deal of damage results from all of this. I am not talking about the misinformation created by their lying, or the injustice done to those who deserve to be recognized, but about something even more serious: that those who work to achieve fame, having lost all hope of being able to attain it, will no longer attempt noble and virtuous deeds, because every undertaking has a definite goal and clearly defined aim and intention. This matter of how much evil and danger can come from poorly written histories is a question that does not even need to be addressed here because even the most simple and naive person is already aware of it. For this reason, I am fearful that modern Castilian history suffers a shortcoming in that it is told with a lack of daring and with an attempt to pacify kings. While it is true that this history comes to us by the hand of Alvar García de Santa María,[3] a notable and discreet man who knows how to compile history and who has the conscience to preserve the truth, it is also true that this history was taken from him and passed on to other hands. With the lawless ambition that is prevalent in our time, it is reasonable to fear that the chronicle is not in the same state of purity and simplicity in which he wrote it.

For this reason, and because I am not skilled in writing in the form and manner of an historian, which I wish I were—and even if I had such skill, I am not as well informed about the events as the task would require that I be—I have decided to write this work somewhat like a registry or memorial to the two kings who reigned in Castilla during my lifetime. I will write of their families and of their lives and of their moral character, and in doing so, I will tell

---

3. Alvar García de Santa María (1349–1445) was author of the *Crónica de Juan II* [Chronicle of Juan II], a text often attributed to Pérez de Guzmán.

of the lineage, the physical attributes, and the qualities of temperament of some of the great lords, prelates, and knights who lived during this time. And if perchance I should include a few brief stories about events that occurred in Castilla during this period, it is out of necessity that I do so, that is, because the material requires it.

I am using as a model a stylistic invention of Guido delle Colonne,[4] who translated the History of Troy from Greek to Latin, and who in the first part of that book wrote about the appearance and deeds of the Greeks and the Trojans who took part in the conquest and defense of Troy.

I shall begin with Don Enrique, the third king by this name to reign in Castilla and Leon, who was the grandson of King Enrique the Noble, the second by that name.

King Enrique, the third by this name, and son of King Juan

King Enrique III was the son of King Juan and Queen Leonor, daughter of King Pedro of Aragón. He descended from a noble and very old and illustrious family of Gothic kings and, of special note, from the glorious Catholic Prince Recaredo, King of the Goths in Spain. According to Castilian history, it seems that the bloodline of the kings of Castilla, from one king to the next, has continued until the present day, that is, more than 800 years, without alteration by any other line or family. I believe that there are very few Christian royal families with such long histories who can claim such notable kings and princes, including five siblings who were saints: St. Isidore; St. Leander; St. Fulgentius; St. Florentina,

---

4. Guido delle Colonne was a Sicilian poet and historian who composed a version of the history of Troy in Latin, which was completed in about 1287. The text was later widely translated throughout Europe.

the nun; and Queen Theodora, mother of King Recaredo, who was considered a very holy woman and who had a martyred son named Hermenegild. In modern times, King Fernando, the king who captured Sevilla, Córdoba, and the entire border region, is considered a saint.

King Enrique began to rule shortly after he reached eleven years of age, and he reigned for sixteen years, so that he lived to be only twenty-seven years of age. He was of medium height and of quite a pleasant disposition. He was fair and blond and had a somewhat turned-up nose. But, when he reached seventeen or eighteen years of age he suffered several bouts of serious illness that weakened his body and damaged his constitution. As a result, he lost the good looks that he at one time had. His illness was even the cause of great changes in his personality, for with the strain and affliction of his lengthy illness he became sad and irritable. He was unpleasant to look at and very hard to talk to, so that most of the time he was solitary and melancholy. And in the judgment of many—whether it was his illness that caused it or a natural predisposition—he seemed more inclined to be capricious than to be sober and mature.

But, even though he did not have an abundance of good sense, he did have some qualities that enabled him to keep his holdings in good order, and his Kingdom reasonably ruled. This was because he believed in his own ability to rule and to govern. And, of course, less effort and good sense are required of kings than of other men to rule because they have access to wise advisors, and because their power is so great, especially the kings of Castilla, who, with even minimal manliness, will be awe-inspiring. And therein lie their presumption and their unwillingness to be governed by others. And so, our King was very feared and also kept himself very isolated, as has already been mentioned. And just as great familiarity and openness breed contempt, likewise, isolation and taciturnity cause a prince to be feared.

This King had a great desire to manage his holdings, to increase his income, and to maintain justice in his Kingdom; and any man who devotes himself so completely to something, by necessity achieves some degree of success. So, how much more a king, who is never at a loss for good ministers and officials to carry out whatever task he desires! This King had some very good and notable clergymen, prelates, and doctors with whom he isolated himself in counsel and with whose advice he managed his financial and legal affairs. And it cannot be denied that he had the prudence to recognize and appoint good people to his Council, which is not an insignificant virtue in a monarch. And so, in such a way, he kept his estate in order and his Kingdom peaceful and tranquil, and in a short period of time built up a great treasury, because he was not very free with his money. And when a king is frugal and prudent, and when he has a high income, he is bound to become rich.

The courage of this King could not be definitively measured because courage becomes apparent only in the practice and execution of military feats, and he never engaged in war or in battles in which his courage could be demonstrated. This was either because his faint-heartedness was so great that one would have to witness it to believe it, or because by nature he was not disposed to engage in war or in battles. And I, submitting my opinion to the discreet judgment of those who have dealt with this question, maintain that it was both of these defects that prevented him from going to war. It is true that he was at one time at war with King Juan of Portugal, and that the year he died he had begun a war with the King of Granada, but he engaged in each of these wars more out of necessity than out of desire.

The war with Portugal happened in this manner: King Juan of Portugal, during a truce, took the city of Badajoz and captured Marshal Garci González de Herrera, who was in that city. The war continued for three years and the King of Portugal was put in a serious predicament, as much by the great men of the King of

Castilla as by the defection of some of his own men to the army of the King of Castilla. If our King had had the desire or the inclination to continue the war, in view of the opportunity presented to him at that time, he would either have taken the Kingdom or would have benefited greatly from the treaty. The Portuguese knights who went over to the side of Castilla in this war were the following: Martín Vázquez de Acuña and his brothers Gil Vázquez and Lope Vázquez; Alvar González Camelo, prior of Ocrato; Juan Fernández Pacheco and his brother Lope Fernández; and Egas Cuello.

In this war the King of Portugal won the city of Túy de Galicia and later besieged the manor of Alcántara.[5] Our King sent his Constable, Don Ruy López Dávalos, there to help. The Constable arrived there from the other side of the River Tajo and gave aid to the manor. And although the King of Portugal had many men there, he saw that he could not take the manor, and he retreated. The Constable of Castilla crossed into Portugal and, spending several days there, caused great destruction. He took by force a very powerful manor that they call Peñamoncor, and from there he returned to Castilla. During that time, Don Gonzalo Núñez de Guzmán, Master of Alcántara; Don Diego Hurtado de Mendoza, Admiral of Castilla; Diego López de Stúñiga, Chief Justice of the King; Pedro Suárez de Quiñones, Chief Governor of León; and other great lords had surrounded Miranda de Duero. The Constable arrived there, and the manor was under such duress that the Portuguese had to forego battle. They requested aid from their King, which was not forthcoming, so they surrendered. Later when the war ended and there was a treaty of peace signed between the two kings, the cities and manors were returned to their respective kingdoms.

5. The word *manor* refers not only to the large medieval residence of a nobleman, but also to all of its surrounding land, which was often so extensive that it might even include villages.

The war with the Moors happened for this reason: the Moors, during a truce, captured a castle called Ayamonte, which belonged to Don Alvar Pérez de Guzmán, Lord of Olvera. The Moors received several mandates from the King to return the castle, but they refused to do it. Despite all of this, some maintain that the King, even then, would not have entered into war against them had it not been for the fact that he had already positioned his border commanders in such a way that the King of Granada, out of fear of war, would come around and do what Don Enrique wanted him to do. But, it happened by the ordinance of our Lord God, who often works contrary to the will of men, that the Moors should enter in great strength through Quesada toward Baeza. And Pedro Manrique, Governor of León, who was border guard of the Bishopric of Jaén, came out to meet them, and with him, Día Sánchez de Benavides, military leader of that same bishopric, and other knights. And although the Moors were in greater numbers, the King's forces fought against them and broke through their lines with great strength and then retreated to a high knoll since night was falling. A number of Moorish knights were killed, and among the Christians killed were Martín de Rojas, brother of Don Sancho de Rojas, Archbishop of Toledo; Juan de Herrera, Marshal of Prince Fernando; Alfonso Dávalos, nephew of Constable Don Ruy López; Garci Álvarez Osorio; and some others. And although in this skirmish neither side declared victory, it is certain that the Governor and his men fought very well as good knights.

And so this battle was the cause of the King's going to war, and of his going to Toledo and gathering all of his people there, and convoking the *Cortes* to provide money and to organize the events of the war.[6] While in Toledo, he was stricken by illness, and he died there on Christmas day, 1407. He left behind his son, Don Juan, who reigned after him; a daughter, Princess Doña María,

6. See note 3 of Introduction.

who is Queen of Aragón; and a daughter, Princess Doña Catalina, who was born only a few days earlier and who later married Prince Enrique. He left Queen Catalina and Prince Fernando, his brother, as guardians of his son, the King.

Queen Catalina, wife of King Enrique, daughter of the Duke of Lancaster, and mother of King Juan

Queen Catalina, wife of this King Enrique, was the daughter of John of Lancaster, legitimate son of King Edward of England, who as a duke married Doña Costanza, daughter of King Pedro of Castilla and Doña María de Padilla.

This queen was tall and very heavyset, fair and rosy and blond. From the size of her body and the way she moved, she looked as much like a man as like a woman. She was very modest and carefully guarded herself and her reputation. She was liberal and generous, but highly influenced and easily swayed by her favorites, a vice that, in general, is very common among monarchs. She was not very well disciplined in her personal habits.

She suffered a lot from palsy, which impeded both her speech and her bodily movements. She died in Valladolid in 1418 at the age of fifty.

Prince Fernando, who was King of Aragón

Prince Fernando lived during the time and reign of his brother King Enrique. The Prince was handsome, quiet, affable, chaste, and honest. He was a very true and devout Christian. His speech was spiritless and lazy, and even all of his actions were slow and lethargic. He was so patient and long-suffering that it seemed that he was not troubled by even the slightest trace of anger or wrath. But, he was a very prudent prince who performed his deeds with good and mature counsel, and who was quite generous with those who served him. But, among all of his virtues, the most praiseworthy were the great humility and obedience that he had always shown to his brother the King, and also the love and loyalty he had for Don Juan, the King's son.

But, despite all of Don Fernando's virtues, King Enrique always kept him in a subordinate and submissive position. This was the case either because all kings are generally suspicious of their brothers or of anyone who is a legitimate descendent of the royal family, or because someone had falsely put some doubts into his mind concerning his brother, the Prince. But, Don Fernando, overlooking his brother's harshness and suspicion, bore it all with great patience and obeyed him with the greatest humility. And although several powerful men in the Kingdom had tempted and coaxed him to assume the throne since his brother, the King, was not a good ruler because of his ill health, he nevertheless refused to do so. He preferred that the ruling of the Kingdom, as well as the decision as to who should do the ruling, be left to the will and the disposition of the Lord. He preferred to wait for God's solution to these two problems rather than to provide some solution himself that might be scandalous and harsh. And so our Lord, who, often even in this life, responds to the good will of men, looked down on the humility and innocence of this prince, and protected him from the suspicions of his brother. And the ruling of the Kingdom, which the Prince did not accept when it was offered to him at that untimely and inopportune moment, was later granted to him by God with the blessings of the King and to the joy of the entire Kingdom. And, as has already been mentioned above, his brother, the King, at the end of his days, named him as guardian of his son, the King and ruler of his Kingdom.

This is a clear example and a noble doctrine to be followed by all princes who are subjects of a king and under his rule! They should look at this lesson as if in a mirror. They should not allow themselves to be motivated by ambition and unbridled greed to rule and to govern, and with no other practical purpose. Nor should they become involved in disturbing the order or in attempting to occupy the royal residence or to take action against the king. Rather, with all obedience and loyalty, they should remain under that yoke placed on their shoulders by God. They should follow the example of that holy and notable King David, when he saw himself pursued by King Saul, who was condemned and cast out by God. Although there were many times when David could have killed him, he drew back from such an act, waiting for the intervention and solution that God might provide. And God will give an answer to those who follow this example, and He will respond to their honest intentions, graciously giving them what they had so virtuously rejected, just as this holy King David had done.

To return to the matter at hand, this noble and Catholic prince, after his brother the King had died, was left, along with Doña Catalina, to be the King's guardian and to govern the Kingdom. For that reason I must therefore briefly relate his noble and virtuous deeds because, as I said at the start, it is not my intention to write history, but to write a memorial or registry about the issues already mentioned. So well and discreetly did Don Fernando behave toward the King, his nephew, and in the governing of the Kingdom, and in honor of the crown of Castilla, that it is with great truth that one can truly point out three of his most outstanding virtues. First, he had great fidelity and loyalty to the King. Second, he maintained great justice in the Kingdom. Third, he brought great honor to the nation.

As everyone is aware, that war with Granada that his brother the King had started out of necessity, the Prince pursued and continued, wishing to do service to God and to bring honor to Castilla.

Looking at his first quality, that is, the fidelity and loyalty he had for the King, his lord and nephew, everyone knows that when the King died and left a twenty-two-month-old heir in the cradle, this child was held in great reverence by the Prince. He served him and obeyed him with the same fervor that he had rendered his father, the King, and he guarded him with the diligence and care that he would have shown for his own son.

As far as the administration of justice in his Kingdom is concerned, I believe that it is proof enough to say that in the ten or more years in which he ruled and governed with the Queen, there was never even a hint that the Kingdom was in a state of guardianship; there was such peace and tranquility throughout the Kingdom! In fact, the people were even more peaceful and serene than during the reign of his brother, the King. And so, exactly how good and discreet his rule was became evident later because, from the time he died until the present, there has never been peace and harmony in the Kingdom. It does not seem to me as if there could be more clear and evident proof of his good governing than the fact that, while he served as guardian to the heir of the throne, the Kingdom was ruled better than it had been during the period between when the King reached his majority and when he attained the perfect age of forty. In the time from his death until the present year, which is 1450, there has been no end to discord and dissention, which has spawned death, imprisonment, exile, and confiscation so well known that I need not write about them here.

And now coming to his third virtuous act: after his brother, the King, had died and the provinces that he and the Queen were to rule were assigned to each of them, he left for the border, which some people were not pleased about. He could not enter into the Kingdom of Granada until the end of September, however, because of an illness that overcame him. For that reason, during this first year, he could do no more than surround the manor of Setenil. And because Setenil was very well fortified, and because winter was coming on, he was not able to take the manor. But he sent men throughout the land, and they did great damage in the Kingdom and won the very noble fortress of Azara, and Pruna, and Cañete, and Ortejícar, and Torre de Alhaquín. And leaving the border guards there, he returned to the King. And then in the third year after his brother, the King, had died, he returned to the war, and in the month of May surrounded the manor of Antequera. While it was surrounded, there arrived there on the side of Granada, two princes, brothers of the Moorish King, who were called Cid Ali and Cidi Hamete, against whom Prince Fernando entered into battle in the area between the two hills that are called Boca del Asna. With the help of God the Moors were defeated.

Sancho de Rojas, Archbishop of Toledo, and Juan de Velasco, Royal Chamberlain, began the battle, because they were positioned on a high cliff on the side through which the Moors were coming and where they were then defeated. The Prince with all of his men went by way of the other side of Antequera, and as he arrived at Boca del Asna, the Moors completely abandoned camp. It has been said that the Moors numbered 5,000 knights and 80,000 infantrymen, and as many as 5,000 of them were killed. And many more of them would have been killed were it not for the fact that the Castilians are easily satisfied with a small victory. The common people joined in a group of twenty men to strip a single Moor, for which reason their advance did not proceed as it should have. And so, the Castilians knew how to win the battle, but not how to follow up on their victory. In this battle a very good knight died who was called Lope Ortíz de Stúñiga, Judge of Seville. When the battle was over the Prince returned to his camp and held Antequera surrounded for more than five months. He took it in the month of October and won other fortresses nearby. He left his servant, a very noble knight named Rodrigo de Narbáez, in charge of the fortress.

Before the Prince left Antequera, he learned that his uncle, King Martín of Aragón, had died leaving no sons—his son, King Martín of Sicily, had died shortly before—and that Fernando himself would succeed to the throne. And for that reason he ended his participation in the war with Granada. If he had not, according to the way things were going in the war, and the willingness he had to continue it, he surely would have been victorious.

And so, after many negotiations, he acquired the Kingdom of Aragón, which the Kingdom of Castilla looked on with great favor. He was provided with many men of arms, and the King, his nephew, gave him monetary help for a year that amounted to forty million.

Some would like to attribute greed to this prince because he procured for his son, the Prince, the grand mastership of Santiago, and for his son, Prince Sancho, the grand mastership of Alcántara. But there is an easy answer for those who raise this question, because it has been shown through experience that every grandee who gains power and privilege takes for himself as much as he can of honors, positions, and vassals.

This King of Aragón died in a place in his Kingdom that they call Igualada, and his death disrupted the peace and harmony of Castilla. He died at the age of thirty-four, and he left his sons, Don Alfonso, who today reigns in Aragón; Don Juan, King of Navarra; Prince Enrique, Master of Santiago; Prince Pedro, who died in the siege of Naples when he was struck by a cannonball; Prince Sancho, who died shortly before his father; and daughters, Doña María, Queen of Castilla; and Doña Leonor, Queen of Portugal. And so his sons and daughters reigned in the four Kingdoms of Spain.

Don Ruy López Dávalos, the Good Constable of Castilla, thus named because of his great goodness

Don Ruy López Dávalos, Constable of Castilla, came from a good family whose ancestral home is in the Kingdom of Navarra. He began with only a small estate. He was a well-built and handsome man, quite happy and charming. His conversation was pleasant and amicable. He was very brave and accomplished great feats in war. He was sensible and discreet. He was quick to make a judgment, but he did so with skill and with attention to detail. He was long-suffering and of a trusting nature.

But, just as in this world there is no person without some fault, he was not very generous, and he also liked to consult astrologers, which is a weakness to which many great men succumb and by which they are deceived.

He was well thought of by King Juan, but he gained such favor and position with Don Juan's son, King Enrique, that there was a time in which all of the affairs of the Kingdom were in his hands. He gained a very large estate and many holdings. He was the third constable of Castilla, because the first was Don Alfonso, Marqués de Villena, son of Prince Pedro of Aragón; the second was Don Pedro, Count of Trastámara, son of Master Don Fadrique; the third is this Ruy López, who ruled Castilla for a time, because he held such favor with King Enrique.

In the war with Portugal, Ruy López accomplished notable military feats. But later, because of the meddling of some who did not like him—and because kings often, when they become adults, lose the love they once had for those who helped bring them to power as children—he became so distanced from the King and found himself so clearly in the King's disfavor that he was at the point of losing his estate and his life. But, either because he was innocent and blameless, or because the King wished to save him, considering all of the services he had rendered, and not to undo in the man all that he had done, the King only took away the favor that Don Ruy López had enjoyed and his power, but he left him with his estate and his honor. And if that was the case, then we can say that the King behaved notably.

But in the end, when the time ordained by our Lord had arrived either to purge him of his sins or to try his patience, and as Castilla was going through a period of diverse and adverse fortune, this notable knight, for fear of being taken prisoner, left for Aragón. Then, by order of the King, all of his assets were taken away from him: his goods, his titles, his manors and lands, and they were divided among the grandees of the Kingdom. And now Ruy López, an old man of seventy, plagued by the gout and other ailments, greatly distressed by the false accusations made against him and by his exile and the loss of his assets, died in Valencia del Cid, leaving his sons and daughters in difficult straits. He had three daughters-in-law: the first, a woman of low lineage; the second, Doña Elvira de Guivara, of a notable line of grandees; the third, Doña Costanza de Tovar, of a good family of knights.

The reason for these losses of his is that he was accused of dealing with the King of Granada in disservice to his King, which surely was a false and malicious accusation, because later it was clearly demonstrated that his secretary, acting under the advice of others, had the letters falsified. When the Secretary was sentenced to death, he confessed the treachery, and so the evil one suffered, but the innocent one received no restitution.[7] From this it appears that Don Ruy López was accused more out of greed for his assets than out of zeal for justice. And so, the avarice that has come into Castilla and that has taken hold of her has destroyed in her all shame and conscience, to the extent that, in our times, it is not the evil man who has enemies, it is the very rich man.

Don Alfonso Enríquez, Admiral of Castilla, and son of the Master of Santiago, Don Fadrique, brother of King Pedro

Don Alfonso Enríquez, Admiral of Castilla, was the illegitimate son of Don Fadrique, Master of Santiago, son of King Alfonso.

---

7. The secretary in question was named Juan García de Guadalajara. His treachery was exposed by the Constable's steward, Alvar Núñez de Herrera, who had been imprisoned as an accomplice to the Constable. Bordona

He was of medium height, fair and ruddy, and stout. He was quick witted, but discreet and attentive to detail. He was quite amusing in his speech. He was frequently driven to impulsive and unpredictable rage. He was quite brave, and he was wont to extend his hospitality to good people. And those who were of the lineage of the King and who did not have as much status found in him both favor and assistance. He had an honored home, set an excellent table, and understood much more than he said. He died in Guadalupe at the age of seventy-five.

Don Pedro López de Ayala, notable knight, Royal Chancellor of Castilla

Don Pedro López de Ayala, Royal Chancellor of Castilla, was a knight of great lineage. On his father's side he descended from the family of Haro, from whom the Ayalas descend. On his mother's side he comes from the Zavallos, which is a great ancestral home of knights. Some from the Ayala family claim that they are descendants of a prince of Aragón who was given the feudal estate of Ayala by the King of Castilla. And I also have seen it written by Fernán Pérez de Ayala, the father of this Don Pedro López de Ayala, but I have not read it in any of the histories nor do I have any sense of certainty about it.

This Don Pedro López de Ayala was tall, thin, and good-looking. He was a man of great discretion and authority, and of great counsel in peace as well as in war. He held a high position among the kings during whose reign he lived. As a young boy he was a favorite of King Pedro, and later, of King Enrique II. He was a counselor of the King and very much admired by him. King Juan and his son Don Enrique made great mention of him and took him into their confidence. He witnessed many great events in both war and peace. He was taken prisoner twice, once in the Battle of Nájera, and again in Aljubarrota.

Pedro López de Ayala had a very sweet disposition, could converse well, and had a strong sense of conscience. He was very much a God-fearing man. He loved learning and he devoted himself to books and to reading history, so much so that, although he was very much a knight of great discretion in worldly matters, he had a natural inclination to study. A great part of his time was spent in reading and studying, not books of Law, but books of philosophy and history. And because of him, certain books are known in Castilla that previously were not, such as the work of Livy, which is the most notable Roman history; the *De casibus virorum illustrium;* the *Moralia* of St. Gregory, the *De Summo Bono* of St. Isidore; the work of Boethius; and the *Historia Troyana*.[8] He compiled a history of Castilla from the time of King Pedro until the time of King Enrique III. He wrote a good book on hunting[9]—he was very much a hunter—and another, *Rimado del Palacio* [Palace verses].[10]

He was very fond of women, more than was fitting for the wise knight that he was. He died in Calahorra in 1407 at the age of seventy-five.

Don Diego López de Stúñiga, Chief Justice of the King

Diego López de Stúñiga, Chief Justice of the King, lived during the time of King Juan and King Enrique III. On his father's side, he came from Astúñiga. The ancestral home of this family is in Navarra. I have heard one member of the family say that the Stúñigas are descendants of the kings of Navarra and, in particu-

---

8. The author refers to Castilian translations of Boccaccio's *De Casibus*; St. Gregory's *Moralia*; St. Isidore's *De Summo Bono*; Boethius' *De Consolatione*; Guido delle Colonne's *Historia Troyana*; and Livy's *Historia Romana*.

9. *The text on hunting was entitled De la caza de las aves e de sus plumajes e melecinamientos [On the hunting of birds and on their types of plumage and their diseases]*

10. *Rimado del Palacio* [Palace verses] is a long poem with didactic elements that contains sections dealing with the Ten Commandments and the Seven Capital Sins, as well as a critical commentary on life and events of the royal court.

lar, of a great man named Íñigo Arista, from whom the kings of Navarra have descended. They say that it is for this reason that there are many in their family named Íñigo. But, I am not certain of this. On his mother's side, this Diego López comes from the de Horozco family, a good family of knights.

Don Diego was a good-looking man of medium height. His face and eyes were dark and his legs were thin. He was reserved in his conversation and was a man of few words but, according to what has been said by those who have chatted with him, he was an intelligent man, one who could arrive at great conclusions with just a few words.

He was a good friend, and he was very much favored by, and very close to, those two kings who reigned during his lifetime. He acquired a large estate, he dressed very well, and even in his old age he loved the women and he dedicated himself to them with free rein.

I have never heard anything about his bravery; that is, I think, because in his time there were no wars or battles in which he could demonstrate it. But, one could presume that a knight of such lineage and such discretion would guard his honor, his reputation, and his name, since all of the labor of bravery at arms goes into that guarding.

Don Diego Hurtado de Mendoza, Admiral of Castilla

Don Diego Hurtado de Mendoza, Admiral of Castilla, was the son of Pedro González de Mendoza, a great lord in Castilla, and of Doña Aldonza de Ayala. The ancestral home of the de Mendozas is in Álava; the family is of an old and great lineage.

I have heard some say that they are descendants of the Cid Ruy Díaz,[11] but I have never seen it in writing. I do remember, however, having read in that chronicle of Castilla that talks about the

---

11. Ruy Díaz is the Christian name of the Spanish national hero, El Cid.

deeds of the Cid, that Queen Urraca, daughter of King Alfonso who won Toledo, was married to Count Don Ramón de Tolosa, by whom she had a son, King Alfonso, and later, that Queen married Don Alfonso of Aragón, who was called "The Warrior." Her marriage with this King was annulled, and she returned to Castilla. And not having guarded her reputation and the integrity of her person as she should have, she dishonored herself with Count Don Pedro de Lara and with Count Don Gómez de Campo de Espina. From the latter count she bore a son named Fernando Hurtado, who, I have heard it said—not that I have ever read it—was an ancestor to the de Mendozas, and that these Hurtados were of this lineage and thus derive their name.

Returning to the subject at hand, this Admiral, Don Diego Hurtado, was small in stature and had a washed-out complexion. He was somewhat snub-nosed, but he had a good and gracious countenance, and his build seemed to indicate that he was quite strong. He was a man of subtle wit. He was quite prudent, very amusing in his manner of speaking, and bold and daring in his words, so much so that King Enrique III complained of the liberties that he took and of his daring.

One cannot say much about his bravery because there were no wars during his lifetime, except for a short time when King Enrique was at war with Portugal. During this war he brought a great fleet of galleys and ships to the coast of Portugal and did much damage there; and in the battles with some manors, he conducted himself well and with great courage.

He loved his family very much, and he was very close to his relatives, more so than any other grandee of his time. He liked very much to construct buildings, and he built some very nice residences. And, although he was not considered very generous, he had a great house of knights and squires. During his time, there was no knight in Castilla who had inherited such wealth. He was very fond of women. He died in Guadalajara at the age of forty.

Gonzalo Núñez de Guzmán, Master of Calatrava, a good knight

Don Gonzalo Núñez de Guzmán, Master of Calatrava, was a great lord in Castilla. His ancestral home is in Canderroa, but its founding and its beginning are in the Kingdom of León, because his family unquestionably comes from Count Don Ramiro. They say that this Count Don Ramiro, either in marriage or otherwise, came together with a daughter of the King of León, and that from their union are descended the members of the Guzmán family. Others tell the story this way: when the kings of Castilla and León recovered land from the control of the Moors, many strangers from other lands came to the conquest, either in service to God or for the sake of chivalry, and many of them stayed. And they say that, among others, there came there a brother of the Duke of Brittany, who was called Goodman, which in their language means "good man." This duke married into the family of Count Don Ramiro and, according to this version of the story, it seems that people were confused by the word "Goodman," and they said "Guzmán." Nevertheless, there is nothing written on this, except what remains in the memory of men. But it would seem that what they say is true because, on the border of the coat of arms of the Guzmán family, there are ermines, which also were used on the coats of arms of the dukes of Brittany. They say that the Almanzas, a great family of grandees, descends from this same Goodman.

The truth and certainty of the origin and birth of the families of Castilla cannot be definitely known, except for what remained in the memory of the ancients. In Castilla, there has always been, and still is, little concern for antiquity, which does no small harm. And on this point one can find many notable examples in history, of which I will relate two. First, during the times in which the Jews had kings, they used to keep in coffers and chests in the temple certain books that told of the events that occurred each year. They were called annals and they contained records on noble families. This custom lasted until the time of King Herod the Great, who, for fear of losing the Kingdom, and for fear that some other royal family might claim it, had all of those books burned. Certainly there was no one among the tyrants who so greatly feared losing his Kingdom as Herod did. And it is for that reason that he ordered the books burned, and he even ordered the death of innocent children, which was an extreme and unparalleled act of cruelty.

The second example from that same time, according to what we read in the Book of Esther, was when King Asuero of Persia kept a book that recorded the services rendered to him and the gifts that he gave in return, without doubt notable acts and worthy of praise.[12]

In Castilla, little attention is paid to the preservation of the memory of the noble lineages and the services done for the king and for the republic. And, to tell the truth, it is hardly necessary to preserve them because, in our time, the noblest man is the richest man. So why would we possibly look at a book of lineages? Wealth determines the nobility of men today. Neither is it necessary to record their services for posterity since kings do not give rewards to the one who best serves them, nor to the one who acts most virtuously, but to the one who most closely bends to their will and pleases them. It would be superfluous and unnecessary to record such matters as wealth and flattery.

Returning to the subject, Master Don Gonzalo Núñez was a very ugly man, heavyset, with a short neck and square shoulders. He was very brave and handled arms very well. He was quick witted, very happy, and excellent company among his own people. He was unaccustomed to being alone; he only knew how to be among his own people.

---

12. See Esther VI, 1

He was very generous, not routinely, but only when he chose to be, and then one could really say that he was lavish. And, in my view, this extreme lavishness, even though it may be a vice, is better than, or less of a vice than, avarice, because many people benefit from the great gifts of a lavish person, and these gifts show the greatness of his heart.

This Master was quite loose in matters pertaining to women. And so, with such virtues and such vices he attained a very large estate and great fame and renown.

There were in his company great men, and some who did not live with him but who received money from him every year. He died at the age of seventy.

Don Juan García Manrique, who was Archbishop of Santiago, and who was a very good man

Don Juan García Manrique was Archbishop of Santiago. The bloodline of the Manriques is one of the finest and oldest in Castilla because they descend from Count Don Manrique, son of Count Pedro de Lara. Notable knights and prelates were part of this family.

This archbishop was a very small man with a large head and big feet. He had good sense but he was not learned. He was very generous, however, and he had a large estate and great relatives who were highly honored. He had a big heart and a lofty and grandiose spirit.

There were often great debates and disputes between the Archbishop and Don Pedro Tenorio, and although Don Pedro Tenorio was not his equal in lineage or in family, he was very learned and good-hearted and had a great deal of dignity. In the end, the Archbishop of Santiago had a falling out with King Enrique III because, by the King's command, Don Fadrique, Duke of Benavente, was imprisoned. The King arrested him when Don Fadrique came to see him in Burgos, which upset the Archbishop very much. And because of this, and because some clerics whom the Archbishop had trusted had informed him that that impostor who was in Rome was the real pope—because at that time there was a schism in the Church—the Archbishop then had dealings with King Juan of Portugal, who was obedient to the Church.[13] King Juan then gave the Archbishop the bishopric of Coimbra, and there he died.

Juan de Velasco, Royal Chamberlain, and son of Don Pedro Fernández de Velasco

Don Juan de Velasco, Royal Chamberlain, was the son of Pedro Fernández de Velasco, a great lord and notable knight. His lineage is great and old and, according to what they say, his ancestors are descended from the family of Fernán González. I have never seen this in writing. It is true, however, that in the history of Fernán González it is said that his son, Count Garci Ferrández, in the *Cortes* that he had established in Burgos, dubbed as knights two brothers named Velasco. Whether these two were relatives of the Count, and whether the Velascos descended from them, history does not tell us.

Juan de Velasco was tall and stout. His face was ruddy and ugly and he had a turned-up, fleshy nose and an awkward body. A very discreet and sensible man, he was quite skilled in managing his home and his estate. His estate was large and he gave lavish parties, surrounding himself with noblemen. He was generous in a methodical sort of way, and he had a great number of knights and

---

13. At this time Castilla was in support of the anti-pope seated in Avignon, who was the Aragonese, Pedro de Luna. Fernán Pérez maintains that the Archbishop mentioned here supported the Castilian position but was later persuaded by others that the true pontiff was the one in Rome. The Archbishop then switched allegiance, left Castilla, and formed an alliance with Juan of Portugal, who had maintained his loyalty to the pope in Rome.

squires. His bravery was not demonstrated very much except that, in the Battle of Antequera, he and Sancho de Rojas were on the front, and he conducted himself quite well there. He died in Tordesillas at the age of fifty.

Don Sancho de Rojas

Don Sancho de Rojas, Archbishop of Toledo, was the son of Juan Martínez de Rojas and Doña María de Rojas, a good and old family of knights. Their ancestral home is in Burueva.

The Archbishop was tall and thin and had a pale complexion, but he was good looking. He had a subtle wit and was very discreet and well educated. He was honest and neat in his appearance and was very charitable. He was a great help to his family and he loved them very much. He was overly sensitive and, as a result, quite vindictive, more so than is fitting for a prelate to be. In the interest of governing and ruling and even of getting revenge, he sometimes resorted to cunning and trickery. In everything else, though, he was an outstanding prelate. He first held the bishopric of Palencia, and later the archbishopric of Toledo. He was favored by, and became close to, King Fernando of Aragón, and with his influence and help he received the archbishopric of Toledo.[14] He died in Alcalá at the age of fifty.

Don Pedro Tenorio, Archbishop of Toledo

Don Pedro Tenorio, Archbishop of Toledo, was a native of Talavera and the son of a knight of slight social stature, but of the good family of the Tenorios. His ancestral home is in Galicia.

---

14. The Archbishop of Toledo was a very powerful figure in the hierarchy of the Spanish Church since he exercised jurisdiction over the largest archbishopric of the Peninsula, which included the bishoprics of Segovia, Palencia, Osma, Sigüenza, Córdoba, Jaén, and Cuenca.

He was tall and attractive, with a turned up nose, a ruddy and pimply complexion, and a powerful voice in which was reflected the bravery and steadfastness of his heart. He was a great doctor and a man of profound understanding. He was very stubborn and harshly stringent, and he even took great pride in these two vices. He was zealous in his pursuit of justice; he was a good Christian; and he was chaste and clean in his person. He was not very generous considering his financial assets. He kept the company of learned men, whose knowledge he took advantage of in important affairs. Among these were Don Gonzalo, Bishop of Segovia, who wrote the *Pelegrina*;[15] Don Viceinte Arias, Bishop of Palencia; Don Juan de Illescas, Bishop of Sigüenza, and his brother, who was Bishop of Burgos; and Juan Alfonso de Madrid, who was a great and famous doctor *in utroque*.[16] This archbishop held a high position with King Juan and with King Enrique, his son, and had great power in the ruling of the Kingdom. But, despite the influence he had with the Kings, he never, either for himself or for a family member, received a vassal from the King; nor did he, despite his great power and intimacy with the Kings, ever fail to visit his bishopric in person. These are two qualities that I think are found in very few prelates of our day. He died in Toledo when he was more than seventy years old.

15. *Pelegrina*, by Gonzalo González de Bustamante, is a legal text surrounded by uncertainty. Although this text is mentioned by contemporaries of Don Gonzalo, the only extant manuscripts by this title were printed in Seville in 1498 and are attributed to Bonifacio Pérez. The two manuscripts, one in the National Library in Madrid and the other in the Escorial Library, are written in Latin. Bordona

16. This is an abbreviated form of the Latin *in utroque jure*; a term used to refer to a scholar who is knowledgeable in civil as well as canon law.

Don Juan Alfonso de Guzmán, Count of Niebla, and a great lord

Juan Alfonso de Guzmán, Count of Niebla, was a great lord in Andalucía. He had a large inheritance and a high income. It is not necessary to speak here of his lineage since enough has already been said in describing Gonzalo Núñez de Guzmán, Master of Calatrava.

He was tall in stature and well built, fair, and blond. He wore his beard rather long. He was very courteous, temperate, and so straightforward and fair with everyone that his estate began to dwindle. Because of his generosity, he was very much loved by the common people who never look below the surface. In Sevilla and in his land, after the King, he was the person who was the most recognized.

He was very generous and very personable with good people, but he was not involved in the *Cortes* or in the palaces of the Kings. Nor was he a man who aspired to rule or to gain influence, but rather he devoted himself to a happy and pleasurable life.

Some considered him lacking in valor, and so with these flaws—and these virtues—and especially because of the great sweetness and kindness of his heart, and for his candor and generosity, the man was well loved. This is not surprising, because these two virtues, clemency and generosity, are very related to one's nature, and they compensate for great defects.

Gómez Manrique, Chief Governor of Castilla

Gómez Manrique, Governor of Castilla, was the illegitimate son of Governor Pedro Manrique, the Elder. The King of Granada held him hostage along with other children of knights of Castilla. And since he was only a child, he was induced and tricked by the Moors to become a Moor himself. When he reached manhood, he recognized the error in which he had been living, and he returned to Castilla and reconciled himself to the Faith.

This Gómez Manrique was of a good height. He had strong limbs, an olive complexion, and was bald. He had a large face and a turned up nose. He was a good knight, sensible, and quite reasonable. He had great courage and was proud and stubborn. He was a good and true friend. He dressed poorly but he kept his house nicely decorated. Although he was true and certain in his deeds, either just for his own amusement or to entertain the people he was with, he would sometimes tell of strange and marvelous things that he had seen in the land of the Moors, which were doubtful and hard to believe.

He died at the age of fifty-five, and lies buried in a monastery called Frey del Val, which he himself had built.

Don Lorenzo Suárez de Figueroa, Master of Santiago

Don Lorenzo Suárez de Figueroa, Master of Santiago, was a native of Galicia, in which province was the ancestral home of his family.

He was tall in stature, stout, and attractive. He was quiet and a man of few words, but he had good sense and good understanding. He kept both his house and his holdings in good order and well run, and for that reason some considered him stingy and greedy. But what he did give, he gave in such a way that his manner of giving made up for the amount that he gave. The small amounts that he did give, he gave secretly, which honors and enhances the gift and makes it more pleasing, because when a gift is given in this way, the one who receives it need not worry about it, and the one who gives it shows that he is not looking for praise.

I have heard nothing about his bravery except that he was diligent in war and in command, which he could not be if he were not brave. He was guided very much by astrologers. He died at the age of sixty-five.

Don Juan González de Avellaneda

Juan González de Avellaneda was a good knight. The ancestral home of his family is in Old Castilla. On his mother's side he was from Fuente Almexir, a notable ancestral home of knights, and from Aza, an ancestral home of grandees. He did not have as great a patrimony and estate as those mentioned above. His vassals numbered two thousand, and his house had one hundred men of arms.[17]

He was a tall, heavy man, stout hearted, strong of limb, proud, and parsimonious. He was a good friend. He died at the age of sixty.

Pedro Afán de Ribera, Chief Governor of the border

Pedro Afán de Ribera was a noble and honorable knight. He lived in Sevilla. On one side of his family he was from the Riveras; on the other side he was of the Sotomayor family. He was chief governor of the border and royal notary of Andalucía.

He was tall in stature, attractive, and had a pleasant face. A man of great authority, he was judicious and, according to what they say, quite brave. And although he did not have a large inheritance of vassals, or as large an estate as the other grandees, he had a big heart, and he thought well of himself, and held himself as an equal to others who had higher rank than he had. He kept his estate in

---

17. Although this sounds like a large number, there were other lords who had much larger estates. For example, the Marquis de Villena, whose estate was considered to be very large, controlled lands on which 150,000 people lived. Álvaro de Luna was lord of lands on which 100,000 people lived (O'Callaghan 610).

good order. He was a man who liked to elaborately entertain others and have many guests. He was very melancholy and at times he was proud. He was very moderate in food and drink. He died at the age of eighty-five.

Marshal Garci González de Herrera, a good knight

Marshal Garci González de Herrera was a good knight. He came from an old lineage of good knights. On his mother's side he was of the Duques, an honorable lineage.

He was tall, thin, and good-looking. He was judicious, brave, generous, and a good friend, but he was melancholy and sad, and rarely seemed happy. For this reason they say that Count Don Sancho, the brother of King Enrique, the Elder, who raised him and loved him very much, used to say that the cloud that hung over Garci González was always there. The Marshal was very much a man of his word. He really loved the women. And it is quite a wonder that a man as sad and grumpy as he was should be so generous and romantic, two qualities that require joy and pleasure. He died in León at the age of seventy.

Juan Hurtado de Mendoza, advisor to King Enrique

Juan Hurtado de Mendoza was an honored knight and advisor to King Enrique III. Of his family and bloodline enough has already been said in the chapter that talks of Admiral Don Diego Hurtado, although the coats of arms of the house of the Admiral and the house of this Juan Hurtado were very different.

This man had a good body and a clean and well-groomed face. Even in his old age, in his person and in his manner, he looked like a knight. He was judicious and had good manners. In matters of arms, I have never heard anything said in his praise or to his detriment. He died in Madrid at the age of seventy-five.

Diego Fernández de Córdoba, Marshal of Castilla

Diego Fernández de Córdoba, Marshal of Castilla, was a well-built, attractive, and brave knight. He was gracious and prudent and so mild-mannered and courteous that he would not utter an angry or harsh word to anyone in the world. He was very clean in the way he dressed, and very careful of what he ate.

His bloodline on his father's side was from Córdoba, from a family of good knights whose origin goes back to the captain of a troop of cavalry raiders, who, without fear of the great effort involved or the risk to his person, scaled the walls of the city of Córdoba, which was a famous and notable feat. And from this man descended many noble knights.

On his mother's side, this Marshal was from the Carillos family, a good and very old line. According to what remains in the memory of some very old men, these knights got there name in the following way: two great German knights who were brothers came to Castilla. Since at that point in time they used to say in Castilla "carillos" for "brothers," the way the commoners do today, they gave them the name Carillos.[18] From these two brothers came later many good and notable knights. This Marshal died at the age of eighty.

Álvar Pérez de Osorio, a man from a great ancestral home

Álvar Pérez de Osorio was a knight from the kingdom of León and had an inheritance of many vassals. The bloodline of the Osorios is great and very old, and, according to history, they come from Count Don Osorio, who was a great lord. I have heard some-

---

18. According to Covarrubias, the word *carillo* was very commonly used in early Spanish to mean "dear one" or "loved one," especially in provincial speech. Bordona

one in this family say that these Osorios come from Saint John Chrysostom, whose name in Latin is *os auri*, which means "mouth of gold." But I never saw it in writing, nor does it seem credible to me, because Saint John "Mouth of Gold" was from Greece and it is not written anywhere that he or any of his family ever passed through Spain. I think, rather, that it was the creation of some clever and inventive man. Since the Latin *os auri* means "mouth of gold," and since the name Osorio sounds close to it, they say that it is all the same thing. I neither confirm nor deny it.

This Álvar Pérez Osorio was tall in stature, ugly, and unkempt, and his assets were poorly organized and poorly administered. From a type of palsy that he suffered, he was left paralyzed on one side of his body, and so he could not walk without leaning on someone. He was very brave, generous, and happy, and, as has already been mentioned, his household was so poorly managed that his estate was diminishing greatly because he spent all of his time in joking and in taking pleasure. He died when he was seventy.

Pedro Suárez de Quiñones, Governor of León and Diego Fernández de Quiñones

Pedro Suárez de Quiñones, Governor of León, was a great and notable knight. The ancestral home of his family is old and good. I have heard some from this bloodline say that the Quiñones descended from a princess who was daughter of the King of León, and on the other side of the family from a great lord named Don Rodrigo Álvarez of Asturias, a lord of Noreña. But I have never read it and, as has already been said, in Castilla they do not make mention of things of this sort, although they should.

This Pedro Suárez was of a good height, bald, and snub-nosed. He was good-looking, brave and wise in war, and discreet and diligent in negotiations. He was very generous, and he liked to have good knights in his house, and he was generous with them. He died at the age of seventy.

He had no legitimate sons, so he left his inheritance to his nephew, the son of his sister, who was a good knight and whom they called Diego Fernández de Quiñones. Special mention is made of him here, not so much because of his estate or because of himself as a person, but because he managed to achieve in this world what few people are able to achieve: great prosperity without great misfortune and tribulation. He inherited nothing from his father, and he had that uncle who left him a large patrimony. And later, he married Doña María de Toledo, daughter of Fernán Álvarez de Toledo and Doña Leonor de Ayala. And if it is true that one of the things that brings a man good fortune is having a good wife, certainly he had been given this blessing, because she was surely among the most honest and noble women of her day. And from her came his second blessing: four good sons who became knights, and six daughters who followed well the good and honest example of their mother, all of whom deservedly married good and noble men.

This Don Diego Fernández had debates and disputes with some of the great men of the Kingdom of León, from which he emerged with considerable honor. At the end of his life he left ten sons and daughters and thirty grandchildren without ever having seen any of them die. He died peacefully and serenely of natural causes when he was more than seventy-five years old. We make note of this here because the life of men is full of trials and tribulations and, for the most part, there is no one, especially anyone who lives a long life, who is not confronted with much adversity and many problems. This knight was indeed fortunate that he never experienced the adversity of Fortune.

Pedro Manrique, Governor of León

Pedro Manrique, Governor of León, was a great and virtuous knight, and because so much about the lineage of the Manriques has already been said, it will suffice to say only that his mother, Doña Juana de Mendoza, was a notable woman.

This Governor was very small in stature and had a long nose. He was very prudent and discreet, and of good judgment and conscience. He was a God-fearing man who had a high regard for good clergymen, and they all, in turn, loved him. He had many good relatives of whom he availed himself when he was in need. He was a man of great courage and he was quite brave. Some judged him to be rebellious and found him to be ambitious to command and to rule. I do not know for certain, but if it were so I would not be at all surprised, because all who feel themselves disposed to and capable of some task or deed are compelled and driven by their own talent to exercise it and to use it because, after all, you will rarely find any man well-prepared for a job that does not take pleasure in doing it. Thus, this knight, because of his great prudence, was sufficiently qualified to rule and govern. Considering that he lived during these confused and immoral times, in which whoever took more, ended up with more, it is not much of a wonder that he too became caught up in it. The truth is this: that in the time of King Juan II, in which there were great and diverse changes, there was not one change in which Manrique was not involved, not in order to do a disservice to the King or to bring harm to the Kingdom, but to be useful and to have power. From such circumstances scandals and misfortunes very often follow. And so, because of the activities in which he was involved, his fortune varied from prosperous to adverse, in that sometimes he held important positions in governing the Kingdom and he increased his holdings and estate, but at other times he endured great tribulations, such as having once been exiled and, at another time, imprisoned.

Some would like to say that he got very close to those relatives that he needed and afterwards forgot them. There were some who criticized him for this. Others excused him saying that he did not have sufficient power and resources to satisfy so many and such great men, or perhaps, even by doing everything in his power, he could not satisfy them. But always he was a good knight and devout Christian and so prudent and wise that Don Sancho de Rojas, Archbishop of Toledo, used to say of him that "what God had denied him in body, He made up for in good sense." He died at the age of fifty-nine.

Don Diego Gómez de Sandoval, Count of Castro

Don Diego Gómez de Sandoval, Count of Castro, Chief Governor of Castilla, was a great knight. His family seat, a good and old ancestral home of knights, is in Treviño.

He was a big man, robust and square-shouldered. He had small eyes and was slow of speech. His actions were sluggish and ponderous; however, he was covetous of advancement and gain. Although he was wise and very brave, in the administration of his home and in financial matters he was negligent and careless. He was not very generous. He was fond of arms and horses. He was a good-natured knight and was without conceit.

When his father died, he was left with very little property, but later the King of Aragón, when he was ruling Castilla, increased his holdings in vassals and posts.[19] And later, the King of Navarra, his son, gave him the earldom of Castro and, in Aragón, the earldoms of Denia and Ayora, and thus he became one of the greatest knights of Castilla. And when Prince Fernando, his lord, claimed the Kingdom of Aragón, this count, leading his troops, along with the other noblemen of Aragón that were following the

---

19. The king referred to is Fernando de Antequera.

Prince, entered the Kingdom of Valencia. There was a battle with the people of Valencia and he conquered them, which was a very notable act. And later, because the affairs of Castilla had passed through the hands of various and diverse factions to the great harm and detriment of the Kingdom, this Count of Castro, following his lord, the King of Navarra, was once captured in the battle of Olmedo and was twice exiled. He lost all of his many holdings, and in this state he died in Aragón at more than seventy years of age. And not only did this noble knight meet with his downfall because of the factions in Castilla, but other very large and some smaller estates were lost. In Castilla, it is easier to win something for the first time than it is to hang onto something you have already won; for many times those fortunes that Castilla has created, she herself destroys.

Don Pablo, Bishop of Burgos, a great sage and notable man

Don Pablo, Bishop of Burgos, was a sage and a man of great learning. He was a native of Burgos, and was a Hebrew who descended from one of that nation's great families. He was converted by the grace of God and by the understanding that he had of the truth, since he was a great scholar in both Christian and Jewish doctrine. Before his conversion he was a great philosopher and theologian; and after he was converted, continuing his study in the court of the Pope at Avignon, [20] he was regarded as a great preacher. He was first, Archdeacon of Treviño; later, Bishop of Cartagena; and finally, Bishop of Burgos. Later, he became royal chancellor of Castilla.

---

20. The author makes reference here to the anti-pope who was seated in Avignon during the time of the Great Schism in the Church, during which the Papacy was split between the pope of Rome and a second pope in Avignon.

He had a very important position with King Enrique III, and he was very much in his favor. And, without doubt, it was with very good reason that he was so loved by every wise king or prince, since he was a great advisor and a very discreet and trustworthy person. He had those great virtues and graces that make a man worthy of the favor of any prudent king. Before Enrique III died, he had appointed him one of the executors of his will, and, after the King's death, he had an important position with Pope Benedict XIII.

Don Pablo was a great preacher. He wrote some very useful texts on our faith, one of which was *Annotations on Nicolás of Lira*; another called *De coena Domini*; a third, *On the family of Jesus Christ*; and a great volume that is called *Scrutinium Scripturarum*, in which, through solid and lively argumentation, he proves that the Messiah has come and that He is God and man.[21]

At this point I am resolved to present some arguments to counter the opinion of those who, indiscreetly and indiscriminately, absolutely and freely, condemn and decry without moderation this nation of New Christians converted in our times, declaring that they are not Christians, and that their conversion is not sincere and legitimate. And to those who thus determinedly and without certain limits and conditions hold to that opinion, I, speaking with all due respect, say that I do not doubt that a people who for generations practiced a certain religion—who were born and were raised in that religion and, all the more so, those who grew old in it and were later by force, without other warnings and exhortations, brought into a new religion—would not thus be faithful and true Christians like those who were born into Christianity and were taught and informed by priests and the Scriptures.

21. His *Adiciones sobre Niculao de Lira* [Annotations on Nicolas of Lira] was published in León in 1545. The first edition of *Scrutinium Scriptuarum* [Scrutiny of the scriptures] appeared in 1470. The texts *Coena Domini* [The Lord's supper] and *Familia Christi* [The family of Jesus Christ] have been lost. Bordona

For even the disciples of our Lord, having heard His holy sermons and having witnessed His great miracles and marvelous works—even they, notwithstanding all that they had seen—forsook Him at the time of His Passion. With little Faith, they doubted in His Resurrection until they were confirmed in the faith by the Holy Spirit. And even later, those who were being newly converted were required, by order of the Apostles, to stop practicing certain rituals of their former religion, until little by little they were strengthened in the Faith.

For all of these reasons, I would not be surprised that there are some, especially women and coarse and dimwitted men that are not educated about their religion, who might not be true Christians. But it is the duty of the most knowledgeable, or even the least learned scholar, to bring the light of the truth to the ignorant person who only believes in the Faith because he inherited it from his father, and not for any other reason. But I do not believe this is true of everyone in general. On the contrary, I believe that there are some devout and good persons among the new converts, and the following reasons bring me to this belief: first, I believe that the holy water of Baptism has such power that it would not be sprinkled and poured on so many without producing some fruit; second, I have known, and do know, among the newly converted some good clerics who, of their own will, live harsh and difficult lives in their religious orders; third, I have seen some of these converted clerics spend much of what is their own money to build monasteries and to reform religious orders that were corrupt and dissolute. I have seen others, in the manner of this bishop and his honorable son, Don Alfonso, Bishop of Burgos, who have written texts of great usefulness to our faith. And if some say that they do these works out of fear of kings and prelates, or to be more pleasing in their eyes and to be worth more to them, my response to these people is the following: in our times, because of our sins, neither the law nor the Faith is regarded with such rigor and zeal that these converts would do this out of fear or out of hope of currying favor. Today it is with gifts and presents, not with virtue and devotion, that the hearts of kings and prelates are won. Furthermore, zeal for the Faith is not so rigorous that, for fear of it, one would cease doing evil and do good.

Therefore, as I see it, a whole race should not be condemned so rashly and absolutely. Yet, I do not deny that new plants or tender grafts require much work, and great care and diligence, until they are well rooted and firmly implanted. And I say furthermore that the children of the first converts should be separated from their parents because the precepts and advice of the parents make a great impression on the hearts of children. And even if, in the long run, it is as those detractors say it is, I still maintain that their conversion was useful and beneficial, because the apostle Saint Paul says, "And so I shall rejoice that the name of Jesus Christ be praised whether it be sincerely or insincerely." Likewise, even if the first generation of converts are not such good Christians, the second and third generations, and even later generations, will be true and firm in the faith. And as proof of this, one can read in the chronicles of Castilla that when the Moors conquered our land because of the sins of King Rodrigo and the treachery of Count Julián,[22] many Christians converted to the faith of the Moors. Their children and grandchildren have defended and still defend this land against us and are very much opposed to our faith. Thus there are as many of these converts in Spain as there are Moors. I have seen in our times that when King Juan II waged war against the Moors, many Moorish knights and, with them, many converts to the Moslem faith[23] passed to our side because of a rift that the

---

22. Count Julian was governor of Septum (Ceuta) in Morocco. Legend has it that his beautiful daughter, Florinda, was ravished by King Rodrigo, the last Visigothic king. In revenge, Julian betrayed the Visigoths to the Moors by aiding them in their invasion of the Peninsula.

23. Fernán Pérez refers to these converts as *elches*, which in Arabic has the pejorative meaning of "turncoat" or "deserter." Bordona

Moors had with their King Esquierdo.[24] Although these converts had ample freedom to convert to our faith, not even one of them did so, because they were already settled and established in the error of their own faith since childhood. Even some of them who died here were already so entrenched in that misbegotten sect, and so imprisoned by their error that, even at the moment of their death, when they no longer had any hope of enjoying worldly pleasures, and when there was no fear of the Moors since they were in Christian territory, they persisted to the last in the evil and obstinate sect in which it was their fate to have been raised and to have grown old. Well, why would I not then think the same possible of the New Christians, judging by what I saw of those Moors? And thus, to my way of thinking, in all of these things we should avoid extremes and be moderate and restrained in our judgments. But if you know some who do not obey the laws of the Church, accuse them before the prelates in such a way that their penalty should serve as a punishment for them and as an example for others. But to condemn all and to accuse none seems to stem more from a desire to speak ill of the offenders than from zeal to correct them.

And returning to our subject, Bishop Don Pablo died at the age of eighty-five. He left two sons who were great scholars: Don Alfonso, Bishop of Burgos and Don Gonzalo, Bishop of Plasencia.

Don Lope de Mendoza, Archbishop of Santiago, and a notable man

Don Lope de Mendoza was first Bishop of Mondoñedo, and later, Archbishop of Santiago. He was a native of Sevilla. People from his birthplace are called "de Mendoza," but they do not have the de Mendoza's coat of arms. It could still be that they are de

---

24. Muhammad VII was called *El Izquierdo,* 'The Left-handed One.' Bordona

Mendozas since, even among the grandees of this family, there is a division and difference in their arms. Some carry a green shield with a red stripe, and others have some panels on their shields. The de Mendozas from whom the Archbishop descends carry a shield having a checkered moon, and I have heard it said that the moon originated with a knight from their birthplace who was named Juan Mate de Luna.[25]

This Archbishop of Santiago was a doctor but was not very grounded in the sciences. He was very gentle, elegant, and could converse pleasantly. His dress was elaborate and his home was very well furnished. The magnificence of his estate was as apparent in his chapel as it was in his chamber and on his table. He dressed exquisitely, such that in adornments and trappings, no prelate of his time was his equal. He was a man of noble and good will, but neither very wise nor loyal. He was tall and well built. He died at nearly eighty years of age.

Don Enrique de Villena, who was the son of Don Pedro, and was Marquis of Villena

Don Enrique de Villena was the son of Don Pedro, son of Don Alfonso, Marquis of Villena, who was later the Duke of Gandía. Don Alfonso, Marquis, was the first Constable of Castilla, and son of Prince Pedro of Aragón. Don Enrique was the son of Doña Juana, illegitimate daughter of King Enrique II, who fathered her by a woman of the de Vega family.

He was a small, heavyset man with a splotched complexion.

---

25. The coat of arms of Don Diego Hurtado de Mendoza had a red band on a green field. The coat of arms of Juan Hurtado de Mendoza displayed ten white panels on a red field. Genealogists assign even a third coat of arms to members of the Mendoza family that settled in Andalucía. Because of the association of this branch of the family with Mateo de Luna, their coat of arms has a checkered gold and black moon on a silver background. Bordona

And as is evident from his life, he was naturally more inclined to the sciences and arts than he was to military life or even to worldly business, either secular or religious. Even in his childhood, when children usually have to be forcefully taken to school, he, without a teacher or anyone else compelling him, was determined to learn, even though his grandfather, the Marquis, wanted him to be a knight and prohibited his schooling. So keen and sharp a wit did he have that he quickly learned whatever science or art he set himself to. It surely seemed that this was a part of his nature, and certainly, a person's nature is very strong, and it is a very difficult and serious matter to resist it without God's special grace.

And moreover, not only was Don Enrique removed and detached from military life, he was even uninterested in affairs of the world, and in the administration of his home, and financial matters. It was astounding how incompetent and inept he was. And because, among the arts and sciences, he particularly favored astrology, some made fun of him saying that he knew a great deal about the heavens, but not much about the earth.[26] And so, with this love that he had for learning, he did not stop at the noble and true sciences, but he allowed himself to delve into some vile and contemptible arts, such as fortune telling and interpreting dreams, sneezes, signs, and other such things,[27] the likes of which are not suitable for a royal prince, much less a true Christian. Because of this, he was held in low esteem by the kings of his time, and in low

26. Bordona suggests that this is a reference to the irregular behavior of Don Enrique's wife, Doña María de Albornoz, and to her relationship with Enrique III, who was Don Enrique's cousin.

27. During the Middle Ages, many attached special significance to sneezing because it was believed that the person who sneezed temporarily took leave of his faculties. This loss was attributed to certain humors rising from the chest to the brain at the moment of the sneeze. Covarrubias considered this a superstition, but those who did believe in it interpreted sneezes based upon the number, time, and circumstances of their occurrence. Other important considerations were whether the sneezer's head was tipped to the left or to the right, and what he was saying, thinking, or doing when he sneezed. Bordona

regard by the knights. Yet he was a very subtle poet and a great historian. He was very knowledgeable and well rounded in many sciences. He spoke many languages.[28] He ate a lot and was very much a ladies' man. He died in Madrid at fifty years of age.

Don Gutierre of Toledo, Archbishop of Sevilla, and later, of Toledo

Don Gutierre of Toledo was first Bishop of Palencia, later, Archbishop of Sevilla and finally, Archbishop of Toledo. He had great ancestors. On his father's side he was descended from a family of great and good knights from Toledo. Some say—and you can even find it in writing, although not in an authentic history—that the family traces its ancestry to a certain count, Don Pedro, brother of the Emperor of Constantinople, who came to Spain to participate in the war against the Moors and in their conquest. On his mother's side, the Archbishop was from the Ayala family.

Don Gutierre was of medium height, had a pleasing face, blue-eyes, and a fair and ruddy complexion. He was very well educated, since he was a doctor. He was a man of great courage, very bold and daring. In the way he moved, in his speech, and in his manners, he seemed more like a knight than a prelate. He was very self-assured and confident, but neither generous nor liberal. He was a good and true Christian. He was quite zealous and good intentioned in his deeds, but his hard and harsh fortune confounded everything. He died at seventy years of age.

Don Alfonso de Robles

Fernán Alfonso de Robles was a native of Mansilla, a village of the Kingdom of León. He was an ignoble man of humble ances-

---

28. Don Enrique was reputed to know not only Italian, French, and some of the other vernacular languages, but also Latin, Arabic, Greek, and Hebrew. Bordona

try. He was stout, of medium height, and he had a sallow complexion. He had a shy and troubled expression. He had good judgment and was quite clever, but he was more inclined by nature toward surliness and malice than toward gentleness and nobility. He was aloof in his dealings with others. He spoke a lot, although very cautiously. But he was very bold and presumptuous about taking command, a typical vice of lower class men who do not know how to stay within their limits and boundaries when they achieve rank. He was a clerk, and later, Leonor López of Córdoba made him Secretary to Queen Catalina, by whom he was held in great favor. So important was he to the Queen that she guided herself and governed her kingdom by no advice other than his.

And so, because of the favor and authority that she bestowed upon him, all the grandees of the Kingdom not only honored him, but you could even say that they obeyed him. These great prelates and knights were men whose ancestors restrained the power of magnificent and noble kings, curbing their unruly wills with good and just boldness for the benefit and advantage of the Kingdom and to protect their rights. That they should now submit themselves to a man of such low social standing caused much shame and confusion in Castilla. And I say it is even more reprehensible and reproachable that, not only did they submit and bow to this lowly man, but these men, whose ancestors would not humble themselves to a lord of Lara or of Vizcaya, even submitted and bowed to a trivial and lowly woman like Leonor López, and to a petty and contemptible man, Fernando López.

For the sake of brevity I shall not mention here the many disdainful and even injurious actions and words that these lowly people directed toward many great and good men. But let the following serve as irrefutable proof and clear evidence of the scarcity of virtue and the excess of greed that characterize our times: great and good men such as these, because of the earnings and profits that they obtained through the intercession of these lowly people, were not able to control their own greed and allowed such people to command and rule, people who, little by ancestry and even less by virtue, deserved it. Having forgotten the noble and memorable words of Fabricio:[29] "I would rather be lord of the rich than be rich," these nobles would rather be servants of the rich than their lords. To illustrate the moral state of the present day, I think it is enough to observe and to consider the administration and rule and good order of Castilla. Because of the sins of her inhabitants, things have come to such a state that each man is honest and good only in so much as his own nature disposes him to be. And each man is defended only in so much as he can defend himself by his own effort and skill, for neither fear of royalty nor the righteous and praiseworthy rigor of princes and lords provides justice in either case.

So, in conclusion, self-interest possesses and rules Castilla today, casting out virtue and humanity. And may the infinite mercy of our Lord put a stop to such a dangerous situation and cure such a pestilential illness. Let it not be the type of cure—better called punishment—that already once, and with justification, remedied the faults and sins of the people of Spain under the rule of two bad kings, Witiza and Rodrigo.[30] In that instance, the Lord used as a scourge on Castilla the evil and perverse Count Julián, by whose aid and counsel the Moors entered Spain. May He, rather, in this case, mercifully instill His grace in her subjects so that, by amending their lives, they might deserve to have good and just kings, since it is because of the people's sins that the king is a bad admin-

---

29. Fabricio was a Roman consul (282 B.C.) known for his honesty and integrity, whose simple lifestyle and absence of greed are being praised here by Pérez de Guzmán. Tate argues that the quote should be attributed to Marcus Curius Donatus. He cites Valerius Maximus, who wrote, "Marcus Curius was an example of temperance for the Romans and a resplendent mirror of strength." When Curius refused riches from the Samnites, he said, "Go back with your leader and tell the Samnites that Marcus Curius would rather be lord of the rich, than be rich himself. Go back with your gift, for as precious as it is, it is full of deceit."

30. Witiza was the Visigothic King (701–710) who was succeeded by Rodrigo, last King of the Visigoths in Spain.

istrator and ruler of his land. Beseech Him in His mercy to enlighten the understanding of the king and to strengthen his heart so that everyone will love and fear him. The misfortune of the present is that the situation is all to the contrary.

Such prominent mention is made here of this Fernán Alfonso de Robles, not because either his ancestry or his nature requires that he be noted among such noble and notable men, but rather to illustrate Castilla's present day vices and faults.

This Fernán Alfonso had great power after twenty years of enjoying the favor of the Queen, as well as the favor of the Constable, Don Álvaro de Luna. But Fortune made her accustomed reversals, and Castilla put into practice the memorable words of the notable knight, Alfonso Fernández Colonel who, when King Pedro ordered him killed, said: "This is Castilla, that makes men and wastes them," with the result that Fernán Alfonso was imprisoned in Valladolid by the King's order, and all his possessions were seized. He died in prison in the castle of Uceda at fifty years of age.

Don Pedro, Count of Trastámara, grandson of King Alfonso

Don Pedro, Count of Trastámara, was the son of Don Fadrique, Master of Santiago, who was the son of King Alfonso and Doña Leonor de Guzmán.

Don Pedro was well built and had a pleasing face. He was somewhat stout. He was very generous and gracious and warm with good people, but, nevertheless, his manner and customs were characteristic of the land in which he lived, that is, Galicia. He was a man who had a great love of women. He was not famous for great bravery; I do not know if it was because of a defect in him or because he did not have the opportunity to prove his bravery. He was the second constable of Castilla.

Don Pedro de Frías, Cardinal of Spain

Don Pedro de Frías, Cardinal of Spain, was a man of humble ancestry, but he achieved great ranking, power, estate, and wealth. He was first, Bishop of Osma, and later, Cardinal. He had a very important position with King Enrique III, who made him an important confidant.

He was a man of medium height with a pleasing face. He was not highly educated. He was very astute and cunning, so much so that he was considered malicious. He was not very devout or honest, nor as clean in his personal appearance as suited his position. He dressed extremely well. He ate with great formality. He greatly enjoyed sensual pleasures, tasty dishes, and fine fragrances.

There were many who complained about the favored position he had with the King, since matters of justice as well as the King's income were all under his control. Important men especially complained about him, claiming that he treated them badly or that, in order to keep the King pleased with his business affairs and income, his actions were harmful to them. In his manner of speech, in the way he moved, in his face, and in the gentleness and sweetness of his words, he seemed as much like a woman as he did a man.

And it happened that at the height of his good fortune, while the King was in Burgos, in his presence, the Cardinal had words with Don Juan de Tordesillas, Bishop of Segovia. On that very same day, the Cardinal's squires struck the Bishop several times. But I have heard the squire who struck the Bishop say that the Cardinal had never ordered it, but that he did it himself, believing that he was serving the Cardinal in doing so. But everyone believed the contrary. And, as I have already said, he was disliked by many, and when they were given the opportunity to do him harm they did not hesitate to take advantage of it. Diego López de Stúñiga, the King's chief justice; Juan de Velasco, the King's royal chamberlain; Don Ruy López Dávalos, his constable; and Gómez Manrique, Governor of Castilla, who at that time was at court, joined together and went to the King at his residence in Miraflores. They presented their complaint about that act so boldly and passionately and they exaggerated the deed to such an extent that the King understood that he must placate them and act on their advice. He ordered Don Pedro—although greatly against his will—to be detained in San Francisco, where he had been staying. And when these great men saw this, they found another way by which to influence the King—making him covetous of Don Pedro's fortune. The idea appealed to the King, and he took 100,000 florins and a large quantity of silver from Don Pedro and ordered him to go to the Pope.

Such was the end and termination of the Cardinal's power, from which the following warning can be drawn: those who have important positions with kings, especially in Castilla where there are constant factions, should use their power with restraint, since when it is lost, they will not be excused for their deeds. When they leave power, they should find more people pleased with them than people complaining about them, and more friends than enemies. In this way, they will not suffer so much, or, if they do suffer, it will not be through their own fault, which is a great consolation to those who are suffering.

King Juan II

Don Juan, the second king of Castilla to have this name, was the son of King Enrique III and Queen Catalina, his wife. He was born in Toro on Friday, the sixth day of March, on St. Tomás' day, in the year of Our Lord, 1405. Twenty-two months after his birth, on Christmas day of 1407, he began his reign, his father having died on that day in the city of Toledo, where King Juan II was then raised to the throne. The following were in attendance: Prince Fernando, his uncle; Don Ruy López Dávalos, Constable of Castilla; Juan de Velasco, the King's Royal Chamberlain; Diego López de Stúñiga, his Minister of Justice; Don Sancho de Rojas, Bishop of

Palencia, later Archbishop of Toledo; and Juan de Illescas, Bishop of Sigüenza. At the time his father died, Juan was in Segovia, where the Queen was keeping him.

By the King's will, the Queen and Prince Fernando were the boy-King's guardians and regents of the Kingdom, while the possession and custody of the King went to Diego López de Stúñiga and Juan de Velaso. But because the Queen felt very offended by this arrangement, and because it did not please the nobles of the Kingdom, the terms were amended and the Queen kept the young King.

A few days after the former King died, Prince Fernando, along with all the knights who were with him, left Toledo for Segovia where the young King was staying. Many important prelates, knights, and representatives of cities and manors went there, and so there was a large gathering of people. There was some discussion between the Queen and the Prince over the form of the regency, but they came to the following agreement: the Queen would govern on that other side of the mountain facing Burgos, and also Córdoba and some other places that were of her administration. The Prince would govern on this side of the mountains facing Toledo and Andalucía, and also Burgos and some other places. After this was agreed upon, the Prince left for the war against the Moors, and with him went all the grandees of the Kingdom. The Queen stayed in Segovia with the King.

What the Prince accomplished in this and the following year in the war against the Moors will not be recounted here because it has already been told above, but I will say that, if the sins of Castilla had not provoked our Lord's indignation to the point of His placing an obstacle in the Prince's way, without doubt this noble prince would have ended this war and would have restored to Spain her former possessions, casting out the Moors and delivering Spain to the Christians. But with the Prince already upon Antequera, having won the battle and having contained the Moors,

King Martín of Aragón died without any offspring, and, by law, Prince Fernando, the son of Queen Leonor of Castilla, King Martín's sister, succeeded to the throne. The Prince had to leave the campaign and tend to the administration of the Kingdom of Aragón. This did great harm to Castilla, not only because of the loss of that conquest, but also because of the absence of the Prince in the governing of the Kingdom, a kingdom that he had governed so peacefully and justly. Unfortunately, just how peacefully and justly he did rule did not become evident until later when, for the lack of good governing, great injuries and misfortunes befell Castilla. It is always true that what is good is recognized only after its opposite appears.

Turning now to speak of this King Juan, you should know that he was tall and had sturdy limbs, but he was not well built nor was he very strong. He was pleasant-looking, fair, blond, and square-shouldered. He had a large face. He spoke quickly. He was a gentle and calm man whose speech was very restrained and plain.

And because his nature was strange and astonishing, I must tell more about it. He was a man who spoke prudently and reasonably, and he had the ability to judge who, among other men, were the best, most prudent, and most elegant speakers. He enjoyed listening to wise and clever men, and he took careful note of what they had to say. He spoke and understood Latin; he read very well; he liked books and stories a great deal. He took great pleasure in listening to poems and he was a good critic of them. He delighted in hearing pleasant thoughts well expressed, and even he himself knew how to turn a good phrase. He was very skilled in the art of riding and hunting and he practiced it often. He was versed in the art of music; he sang and played well. Even in jousting and equestrian games he handled himself well.[31]

---

31. The games referred to here were called in Spanish *juegos de cañas*, and involved a type of jousting with reed spears.

But, although it is true that he was reasonably endowed in these graces, he was sorely deficient in other graces that are truly virtues and that are necessary to all men and especially to kings. After all, the principal virtue of a king, after his religious faith, is to be industrious and diligent in the governing and ruling of his Kingdom. This is proven by the example of the wisest of all kings, Solomon, who, when God told him to ask for what he wanted, demanded nothing more than the intelligence to rule and bring order to his people. His petition so pleased our Lord that He granted him those and other exceptional virtues. King Juan II was so lacking and deficient in this virtue that, despite all the aforementioned talents that he possessed, never for one single hour did he try to attend to or to work at the art of governing. The number of revolts that occurred, and the factions that existed in his time, and the amount of harm, evil, and danger that resulted therefrom had not been seen in the Kingdom under any other king for more than 200 years. And now these problems were so rampant that this King, his reputation, and his Kingdom were in great danger. So great was this King's negligence and disregard for the governing of the Kingdom that he never even attempted to work at it; instead he dedicated himself to activities that were more pleasurable and delightful than they were useful and honorable.

One finds in written histories, at least in the ones that I have read, the ills and wrongs that have come to both kings and their kingdoms because of the kings' negligence and disregard. And so, even many of his own knights and clerics warned King Juan that he and his Kingdom were in great danger because he did not attend to his Kingdom's administration. They also warned him that his reputation was suffering because of it. Furthermore, they advised him that an even more serious consequence was that his conscience was burdened with this and that he would have to give God strict account of the evil that had come to his subjects because of the inadequacy of his administration. They hoped that God would grant him the prudence and intelligence to realize it.

With all this, and although he himself saw how little he was obeyed, and with how little respect he was treated, and in what little regard his decrees and orders were held, he never, not for one day, lifted a finger or devoted his energy to the ordering of his estate or to the governing of his Kingdom. Rather, he left his constable in charge of it all. He put so much confidence in him that to those who did not witness it, it would seem incredible and, to those who did witness it, it was a strange and astounding situation. Regarding matters of the King's income, his treasures, the posts of his household, and in matters of justice in his Kingdom, everything was done according to the Constable's decrees, and nothing was done without his order. Although it is true that decrees, ordinances, pardons, royal favors, and properties were granted in the name of the King and signed with his name, the reality of it was that none of these things happened if the Constable did not wish it to be so: the secretaries did not draft them, the King did not sign them, nor did the Chancellor seal them. Letters were not considered valid, and they were not enforced, without the Constable's approval.

So great and so exceptional was the confidence that the King had in the Constable, and so great and excessive was the Constable's power, that you could rarely find any king or prince, however feared and obeyed he might be in his own kingdom, who was more feared and more closely obeyed than was this Constable. Nor could you find any king or prince who so freely ruled and governed as this Constable did. Not only did he control the posts, the estates, and the favors that the King could provide, but he controlled the ecclesiastical posts and benefices as well. There was no one in the Kingdom who would dare petition the Pope for, or even accept from him, a decree done *propio motu* without the consent of the Constable.[32] Thus, both temporal and spiritual affairs were in his

---

32. *Propio motu*, meaning "by his own hand," is a Latin expression used to describe an action done by someone personally.

hands. The King's only authority was in the signing of royal ordinances, but the issuing and execution of them rested with the Constable. The Constable's power grew so great, and the King's efficacy diminished so much, that no one came to the King to ask for a favor or to offer thanks for a favor granted. From the most important job to the smallest petition, all requests and thanks were rendered to the Constable.

One might find it even more astounding—and, indeed, it has been said—that even concerning natural functions, the King followed the orders of the Constable. Although the King was a young man of healthy constitution and had a young and beautiful queen, if the Constable would tell him not to, the King would not sleep in the Queen's chambers, nor would he give his attentions to other women even though he was, by nature, quite inclined to do so.

In conclusion, we should note two very astonishing facts here. First, this King was excellently skilled in many things, yet he was completely remiss and negligent in the governing of his Kingdom. Neither good sense, nor the experience derived from the many tribulations that he encountered in the struggles and revolts that occurred in his Kingdom, nor the warnings or advice of great knights and clerics who spoke to him of it—none of this moved or stimulated him to act. Even more astonishing was the fact that not even his natural inclination was strong or dominant enough in him to prevent him from submitting to the Constable's orders and advice in all matters and without moderation. And he did so more obediently and humbly than any son ever did to his father, or any cleric ever did to his abbot or prior. There were some who observed this very special love and excessive confidence and took it to be the result of magic and evil spells, but regarding this, there was nothing certain, although there was some indication of it.

The second astonishing fact that we should note here is that a knight, without family and with such a humble beginning, should have such singular power in such a great kingdom. How could the

Constable have attained this power in a kingdom where there were so many powerful knights and at a time when the King was so little feared and obeyed? Even if we were to say that granting this power was within the King's right, how could he give to someone else the power that he himself did not have? To put it another way, how can it be that the deputy is obeyed when the one who put him in that position cannot find anyone that obeys him? Truly, I think that one cannot clearly explain all of this; only He who gave the King such a strange nature could give an explanation for the Constable's power. I do not know which of these two things is stranger: the nature of the King, or the power of the Constable.

During King Juan's time, there were more important and strange happenings than there were good happenings worthy of remembering or useful and beneficial to the Kingdom. Thus it was that when King Juan's uncle, King Fernando of Aragón, died, peace and harmony also died in Castilla. With the death of Queen Catalina, the King's mother, many of the Kingdom's grandees met in Valladolid. They included the following: the Prince, Don Enrique, Master of Santiago; Don Sancho de Rojas, Archbishop of Toledo; Don Alfonso Enríquez, Admiral of Castilla; Don Ruy López Dávalos, Constable; Don Juan de Velasco, the King's Royal Chamberlain; Pedro Manrique, Chief Governor of Castilla; and many other nobles of the Kingdom. And by the common consent and agreement of them all, they removed the King from the house near San Pablo where the Queen had kept him for more than six years, because of her fear that they would take him from her. And on the day that the King left that place, it seemed that he was born again. Just as on the day of his birth he saw the light of day, likewise, on the day that he left that dwelling, he saw his Kingdom and met his people, whom he had previously known only through the guards that were with him there, or when some knight came to pay his respects to him. When he left that place they took him to Tordesillas. Don Sancho de Rojas, Archbishop of Toledo; Admiral Don

Alfonso Enríquez; Constable Don Ruy López Dávalos; and Governor Pedro Manrique were the principal men who governed and ruled the Kingdom. The Princes Don Juan and Don Enrique, sons of King Fernando of Aragón, were there also, but they were very young men and were afflicted with that royal malady that is common and prevalent among young royalty who are ruled and governed by tutors and teachers. There are even some among them who are never cured of this ailment. There were other great men there as well, but everything that was done was accomplished by these four men.

From Tordesillas they went to Medina del Campo, and there the King was married to Princess Doña María, daughter of King Fernando de Aragón. From there he went to Madrid, where he took over the governing of his Kingdom, since he had turned fourteen and had come of age. Since all of the grandees and all of the representatives were there all together, there was a great celebration and great solemnity. And albeit the governing of his Kingdom was handed over to him there, one could better say that he, following his natural inclination toward remissness and almost monstrous negligence, reigned by guardianship rather than by royal rule or administration. Thus he had the royal title and name, but did not perform the acts or the works of a king. For almost forty-seven years, from the day his father died until the day he himself died in Valladolid, he bore no resemblance whatsoever to a king, but rather, he himself was always ruled or governed. Even after the death of his constable, Don Álvaro de Luna, whom he outlived by little more than a year, the King continued to be ruled and governed by others, such as Don Lope de Barientos, Bishop of Cuenca; Fray Gonzalo de Illescas, Prior of Guadalupe; and even some lowly men of little worth. And if, after the Constable's death, he showed some strength or vigor, it was not in ruling or restoring his lands or in repairing the evil and harm that had come to them during the forty-seven years in which he had held the name and title of king, but rather it manifested itself in the desire to accumulate wealth, to which pursuit he gave himself wholeheartedly.

While he was in Valladolid, he was ill with double quartan, which lasted many days,[33] and, according to what was said, he exercised little self-control since he was a big eater and not well-disciplined. And although he overcame the illness, he never regained his good health. He continued his poor regimen, and he had some serious fainting spells, and then died in Valladolid on July 22, 1454. He was buried in the monastery of Miraflores, which he had built for Carthusian friars.

Slightly more than a year before his death, King Juan took an action that surprised everyone. He took this action, some believed, because he had been piqued and stimulated by the will of God. Or was it because his constable had him more in his power and more constrained than he had ever had him? At that point, the Constable did not give him rein to do anything he wanted to do. There were always people under the Constable's command nearby to prevent the King from doing or saying anything. Furthermore, it is said that the service and maintenance of the King's table was so poor and meager that it drew comments from everyone. The Constable did not even allow the King to be with his wife, the second queen, or to have relations with her when he wanted to. Perhaps these are the reasons for the King's actions, or, what is more likely, it was as St. Augustine said of the Amorite:[34] once the Amorite's greed had reached such a point, Divine Justice could no longer, and should no longer, tolerate or suffer that greed. Likewise, it could not suffer or tolerate the Constable's tyranny and usurpation of the Kingdom.

While the King was in Burgos, the Constable resented the fact

33. The quartan is an illness characterized by a fever that recurs every fourth day. In the double quartan, mentioned in this text, the fever recurs every two days.
34. The Amorites were an ancient Semitic people of Mesopotamia, Syria, and Palestine who were a dominant force in the history of these areas from 2000 to

that Alonso Pérez de Vivero had dealings with the King concerning Don Álvaro's estrangement and undoing. Alonso Pérez de Vivero was a man that the Constable had raised from nothing and had made an important man, and to whom the Constable had given an important position close to the King. And now the Constable could not tolerate the relationship that he himself had created between these two men. On Good Friday, the Constable ordered Alonso Pérez to come to his house, and he had him killed. What a very inopportune day for such an act! And later, on the Wednesday within the octave of Easter, which should have been a day of Resurrection, our Lord chose to perform another act; and that day became the day of the Constable's Passion. So to the great amazement—and you could even say incredulity—of the entire Kingdom, the King ordered that Don Álvaro de Stúñiga, later Count of Plasencia, arrest the Constable. The King took from him everything the Constable had there. Then the King took the Constable with him to Valladolid and ordered that he be put in irons in a wooden cage in Portillo.[35]

What can we say here? We can only fear and obey God's unfathomable mandates without interpreting them. Who could understand how a king who, until the age of forty-seven, was so submissively and obediently in the Constable's power that he did not so much as twitch an eyebrow in a show of disagreement, should now suddenly and so abruptly arrest him and put him in chains? We should note that the royal Princes, the King of Navarra and Prince Enrique, with the consent and support of all of the grandees in the Kingdom, had often tried to separate the Constable from the

---

1600 B.C. We were not able to locate the reference to the story about the Amorite cited in this text and attributed to St. Augustine.

35. Fernán Pérez provides the only written testimony that the Constable was ever pent up in a wooden cage, for which reason historians doubt the truth of it. But according to León Corral, in a study published in 1915 in Valladolid, certain witnesses who testified at the trial of Don Álvaro claim that it is true. Bordona

King and had tried to destroy him. They were not only unable to destroy him, but they all, or at least most of them, ended up being the losers. Perhaps it was because they were motivated by their own self-interest rather than by good intentions. But if we want to credit the King for this act, it would seem that we should not, for after the Constable's death, the King was as remiss and negligent as he had been before. He performed no act of power or strength to show himself more a man than he had been before. Therefore, we must believe that this was solely an act of God, since as the Holy Scriptures say, "He alone performs such wonders."

Now, returning to our subject, while the Constable was held at Portillo, the King went to Escalona to take possession of the Constable's manor and the wealth that was there. While the King was in that region, he took legal action against the Constable because of some information that he had received. With the advice of the legal experts in his court, he ordered the Constable beheaded. Thus, the Constable was taken from Portillo to Valladolid and, as prescribed by law, he was there publicly beheaded. It is said that he came to his death more with valor than with devoutness, for his actions and his words on that day served his reputation more than they showed his reverence.

In the opinion of those who knew him, King Juan II was by nature greedy, lustful, and even vindictive, but he did not have the courage to act on those impulses. In the judgment of many, this King's strange ways and nature, and the ills that beset his Kingdom because of them, are attributable to the sins of the Kingdom's inhabitants, since, as the Holy Scripture proclaims, God places the hypocrite on the throne because of the people's sins. And truly, anyone who knew him well and who really thought about it would see that the King's strange nature, and the evils that resulted from it, were caused by the great sins of the people.

This King left a son, Prince Enrique, who rules today, as well as Prince Alfonso and Princess Isabel.

Don Álvaro de Luna

Don Álvaro de Luna, Master of Santiago and Constable of Castilla, was the illegitimate son of Álvaro de Luna, a noble and good knight. The de Luna family is one of the greatest in the Kingdom of Aragón. Many notable persons come from this family, knights as well as clerics, among whom is the venerable and wise Apostolic Father, Don Pedro de Luna, Pope Benedict XIII. All of the de Luna family served the Kingdom of Castilla well. Upon his father's death, Don Álvaro, then a young boy, was left in a very humble and poor condition. He spent some time in the care of his uncle, Don Pedro de Luna, Archbishop of Toledo. And when the Archbishop died, Don Álvaro, still a very young man, was left in the house of King Juan, whose excessive and astonishing love for him has already been described.

You should know that the Constable was small in stature and had a small face, but he was well proportioned and strong. He was a good rider, and was quite skilled in using weapons and participating in war games. He was well informed about palace politics. He was very elegant and had good judgment, although he hesitated somewhat in his speech. He was very discreet. He was quite the deceiver, a great pretender, and was very cunning. He took pleasure in using these arts and in using his craftiness, so it seems that these were a part of his nature. He was considered very valiant, although there was not much chance for him to show his valor with weapons. But when the opportunity presented itself, he did demonstrate great courage. In palace disputes and debates, which require a different type of courage, he proved himself quite a man. He prided himself a great deal on his ancestry, forgetting about the humble and lowly side of his maternal lineage.[36] He had enough courage

---

36. The mother of Don Álvaro was María de Urazandi, who was called *La Cañeta* because she was from a town near Cuenca called Cañete. Bordona

and daring to accept and use the great power that he had attained, either because he remained in power for so long that it had become second nature to him, or because his daring and his conceit were so great that he exercised more a king's authority than a knight's.

It cannot be denied that he had all the ability in the world. And he liked to discuss his affairs with trustworthy men, and he showed his appreciation with deeds for the good advice that they had given him. He interceded for many with the King and, through his intercession, they received favors and great benefices. And if he harmed many people, he also pardoned many who had done great wrongs to him. He was extremely greedy to acquire both vassals and wealth. And just as those who suffer from dropsy can never quench their thirst, he could never satisfy his desire to acquire and possess more. His insatiable greed was never satisfied. On the day that the King would give him—or, more to the point, that he would take—a great manor or honor, on that very same day he would also take from the King a much lesser honor or position if it were to become vacant. So, although he desired valuable things, he did not disdain things of lesser worth either.

One cannot clearly explain or communicate how great his greed was. From being poor and bereft of all possessions when his father died, on the day of his own death he possessed 20,000 vassals, without counting the Order of Santiago, of which he was Master, and other positions that he held. He also had great quantities of *maravedís*[37] in his accounts. It is believed that his income approached 100,000 *doblas*, without counting the unexpected amounts that he received from the King and from treasurers and from tax collectors, which was a lot of money and came from many sources. Although the exact amount of his fortune cannot be known due to

---

37. The *maravedí* was a gold coin minted for the first time in 1172 by Alfonso VIII. It takes its name from the *dinares almorávides*, coins used by the Moors that served as a model for the design of the Spanish *maravedí*. The maravedí was equivalent to one sixth of a Roman ounce and weighed 3.9 grams. It suffered many fluctuations in val-

his imprisonment and the circumstances of his death, it seems that, because of the intense flame of his insatiable covetousness, and because of the way he acquired wealth and held onto it, each day his wealth grew greater. He amassed so great a fortune that it is said that he alone had more wealth than all the great men and prelates of Spain. He just had to have any manor or possession that was close to one of his, and he would either buy it or barter for it. Thus, his holdings grew and spread like a pestilence to nearby places. Likewise, he owned properties and possessions of religious orders and churches by means of exchanges and sales that no one dared to oppose. And the best of this is that, by means of these sales and exchanges, the King paid for it all. He saw to it that many church positions went to his relatives, despite their unworthiness or incompetence. The Pope never denied a request of his and thus his brother had a church in Sevilla, and later in Toledo, and his young nephew had one in Santiago. Who could estimate the degree of his greed and power? For twenty of the thirty-two years that he governed and ruled the Kingdom, there was no temporal or spiritual act executed except by his hand and with his consent.

Only in two situations did fortune go against him. First, it cannot be denied that he did a lot of good and helped many people. Some of them, however, showed him little gratitude, that is, some for whom he did great good afforded him small thanks. Second, he was not fortunate with his children in that one of his sons was quite indiscreet.[38]

If his greed for manors, vassals, and riches was great, no less was

---

ue and in its metallic content over the centuries, but we do know that when Ferdinand and Isabel readjusted the value of currency in 1497, the following equivalencies were established: the *dobla* was equal to 435 *maravedís;* the *florin* was equal to 250 *maravedís;* the silver *real,* to 30 *maravedís;* and one *maravedí* was equal to 3 *blancas.* To translate these equivalencies into current values would be extremely difficult.

38. The Constable had two sons, one by Doña Margarita Manuel, and the other

his ambition to receive honors and distinctions. Not one small thing that he could acquire did he pass up. Once a friend wrote to him that he should be moderate in how much he acquired, but Álvaro de Luna responded with that evangelical authority: *Qui venid ad me non eiciam foras,* or "What comes my way I will not cast away."[39] When our Lord said this, however, it was not with the same intention. Don Álvaro de Luna exercised such diligence and care in keeping and holding his power and the King's favor that it seemed he would not relinquish it even to God. And so, if the King showed good will to someone, that person was thrown out. De Luna allowed only those whom he trusted to be close to the King.

This Constable was very suspicious by nature and he became even more suspicious due to the position he held, since there were many who were envious of him and wanted to be in his situation. Thus, being suspicious and fearful, he easily believed whatever was said to him—and there was no scarcity of those who spread rumors, since flatterers and rumormongers always attach themselves to great men. And so he had the King confiscate property, imprison and exile many men, and even execute some. He always received great support for these deeds because there were many people who were eager to help redistribute a victim's properties. Thus, that old and praiseworthy Castilian custom had come to such a point that one would consent to the imprisonment, or even to the death, of a friend or relative just to acquire the spoils. But, although some deaths resulted from these actions that the King undertook at the Constable's urgings, I do not want to lie, or give him responsibility or blame when he should not have it. I have heard some say, who were in a position to know, that if they real-

---

by Doña Juana Pimentel. The first was Pedro de Luna, Lord of Fuentidueña, who was the Constable's favorite; the second was Juan de Luna, second count of Santisteban. Bordona.

39. See John VI, 37

ly wanted to tell the truth, they would say that de Luna hindered some of the executions that the King, who by nature was cruel and vindictive, had wanted to carry out. I can easily bring myself to believe this opinion.

Greed for advancement and gain caused great and terrible harm during this time, not only to property and people, but, what is more painful and lamentable, to the practice and exercise of virtue and honesty among people. Moreover, people put honesty and shame aside, and with rancor and the desire for vengeance, they allowed themselves to rush headlong toward grave vices.

This was fertile ground for deceit, malice, falsehood, trickery, false oaths, and contracts, as well as many and diverse acts of cunning and evil arts. The greatest deceit and harm done was through false oaths and deceitful marriages, since a surer means of deceit could not be found.

Although the King's remiss and negligent nature and the Constable's excessive greed and ambition were the principal causes of the harm that came to Spain, I will not remain silent about another cause. In this case, the greed of the great knights is not to be pardoned. These knights, in order to increase and augment their estates and incomes, set aside their consciences and their love for their country, and allowed this damage to happen. Furthermore, I do not doubt that they were happy to have such a king, because in this turbulent and unsettled time, when they went fishing in the muddy river, their catch was abundant.[40] Some plotted against the Constable, saying that he had the King deceived or, some even said, bewitched. But they were not motivated by zeal or love of the Republic. Rather their true intention was to gain and occupy the Constable's position. Who could possibly relate or write about all of the injustices that ensued? Insults, factions, imprisonment, ban-

---

40. There is a Spanish proverb that states, *A río vuelto, ganancia de pescadores*, 'The muddy river is a boon to fishermen.' Tate

ishment, confiscation of property, deaths, general destruction of the land, usurpation of positions, disturbances of the peace, injustices, robberies, and wars against the Moors. I would say that for thirty years the evil and harmful deeds never ceased. I will tell about a few of the many to whom harm was done.

In this confusing and turbulent time, the noble Prince Enrique, Master of Santiago, son of the most illustrious Don Fernando, King of Aragón, was imprisoned. Governor Pedro Manrique and along with him two good knights, his relatives Gómez de Benavides and Lope de Rojas, were exiled. Don Ruy López Dávalos, Constable of Castilla, was exiled and died in exile, losing all of his patrimony. Don García Ferrández Manrique, Count of Castañeda; Fernán Alfonso de Robles; Duke Fadrique; and Count Fadrique de Luna were imprisoned. The latter two died in prison, not of natural causes, according to what some say. Later, Don Gutierre of Toledo, Archbishop of Toledo; his nephew, Don Fernando Álvarez of Toledo, Count of Alva; and along with them Fernán Pérez de Guzmán and Garci Sánchez d'Alvarado were imprisoned. Don Juan de Sotomayor lost the office of Master of Alcántara and was exiled. Mosén Diego de Vadillo, warden of the arsenals, was imprisoned. The Bishop of Segovia and Pero Niño, who later became a count, were exiled. The Count of Castro and Fernán López de Saldaña were imprisoned. Fernán López de Saldaña was later freed and then banished. He died in exile. Also imprisoned was the Governor of Galicia. The Count of Alva, the Count of Benavente, and Pedro Quiñones and his brother, Suero de Quiñones, were imprisoned for a second time. In addition, Don Enrique, the brother of Admiral Fadrique, was imprisoned twice. The Admiral himself, Don Fadrique, and the Count of Castro were exiled. Garci Sánchez d'Alvarado was sentenced to death. The noble Princes, the King of Navarra and Prince Enrique, were exiled for a second time and their patrimonies were again redistributed.

Who would be up to the task of telling and relating all of the sad and painful events that occurred in hapless Spain? In the opinion of many, the sins of the inhabitants of Spain caused this state of affairs, while the King's remiss and negligent nature, the Constable's greed and boundless ambition, and, in some part, the behavior of the great lords and knights contributed to the situation as well. But it cannot be denied—and history confirms this—that Spain's affairs have always been unstable and changeable, and they have been without scandal and dishonor for only very short periods of time. But there never had been a time in which a scandalous situation lasted as long as this one did; never one that lasted for forty years; never one with a king who allowed himself to be ruled, without himself governing during his entire life; never one with a favorite who exercised such excessive power for so long. There were some, either ill-intentioned or lacking in good judgment, who tried to defame the King of Navarra and Prince Enrique, and along with them, the Admiral and Count of Castro, the Count of Benavente and Governor Pedro Manrique, as well as many others who followed them. These defamers said that this group tried to kill the King and to usurp the Kingdom, but this was doubtless only malice and falsehood.

But let us forget what was said and just look at the events, which frequently better show the fact of the matter. Everyone knows that when the King was in Tordesillas, Prince Enrique; Constable Don Ruy López; Don García Ferrández Manrique, Count of Castañeda; and Governor Pedro Manrique entered his palace, which was the first offense they committed. They took control of the palace and forcibly removed Juan Hurtado de Mendoza, the King's chief steward, who was very close to the King at that time. They allowed Don Álvaro de Luna, who later became constable, to stay there. They remained with the King for more than seven months. If they had wanted to do any harm, they had ample opportunity. But, to the contrary, they left Álvaro de Luna there to please the King. The King got married in Ávila and he was always regarded as their king and their rightful lord. And later when the King of Navarra and the Prince and all of the Kingdom's nobles met in Valladolid and declared that the Constable should leave the court, they controlled the King for nearly a year. If they had wanted to commit some act of disloyalty, they had every opportunity and were free to do it. Rather, judging by their actions, they treated him with the stateliness and reverence that was due him, and served him and pleased him as they could. It is true that the King was not pleased or satisfied, since they had separated him from the Constable. And later, for a period of time when they were in Castronuño, the aforementioned lords, the King and the Prince; Governor Pedro Manrique; and the Marquis of Santillana; and the Admiral; and Don Gutierre of Toledo, Archbishop of Sevilla; and the Count of Benavente; and the Count of Plasencia; and other great lords, along with the Count of Haro, forced the Constable to leave the court. They kept the King under their control for more than a year, serving him and treating him like their king.

Likewise, in Medina del Campo, they scandalously and in great strength entered his manor by force of arms. This was the greatest and most serious affront committed up to that time. But even then, the King was always held and treated with humble respect. And in such a time, when men of arms usually act more from pride and with little moderation, they kissed his hand and honored him with the respect due him. Even after such an extreme act, he was never in any danger. Later, in Rámaga, near Madrigal, the King of Navarra and the Admiral and Count of Benavente, by authority of Prince Enrique, who later became king, seized Alonso Pérez de Vivero, the King's royal tax collector. Again, they took control of the palace and they stayed with the King in Tordesillas for a year, and all the while protected the King's honor and person.

It is true that the King alleged that all of this was harmful and dangerous to him, since he could not meet with the Constable. All the differences of opinion came to this: the King said that he wanted to be free, while the King of Navarra and the Prince, and those nobles who shared their opinion, said they would be happy to grant the King his physical freedom and also grant him his freedom of choice, which was oppressed by, and subject to, the Constable. When the King could show them that his will was indeed free from the oppression of the Constable, and that as king and lord he would be fair to all, then they would be happy to leave him. But the King said that he would have a free will if they would just leave him alone.

And through all of this controversy, the Kingdom suffered and wasted away. But during these times one cannot honestly say that the King was ever, by threat or by deed, in any danger. But the truth of the matter, all other opinions to the contrary, is this: the princes and the nobles who followed them insisted that they did this to free the King from the Constable's power so that the King, with the aid of good advisors, might rule and govern the Kingdom on his own, following good advice. They further insisted that they did it for love of the Republic and for the love, good, and benefit of all. Their true intention—begging your pardon—was to occupy and fill the Constable's position. They saw that the King was more a man to be ruled than a man who ruled. They believed that whosoever took control over him would rule not only the King, but also the Kingdom, and would increase his own estates and dwellings. They realized that, with the Constable there, they could not accomplish this. Thus, they worked to remove him. Add to this the rancor and enmity that some of these nobles felt for one another, and you will see that they engaged in these affronts to have more than the others, and even to cause them harm. Since they did not have good intentions—their intention was neither to serve God nor to serve their King—nor were they motivated by love of country, they did not meet with success. Rather, these affronts caused the wasting away and destruction of the Kingdom, and, as I have already mentioned, many of these men lost everything.

Although the reasons for God's actions may be hidden and concealed from us, and, because we do not understand them, seem senseless to us, the person who really wants to think about, speculate on, and ponder over them will clearly see that great undertakings and actions never come to a good end if they are not undertaken with good and righteous intentions.

Consequently, I would easily pardon these lords, the princes, and the knights who followed them or who advised them, and excuse them of disloyalty or oppression of the King and the Crown, since I believe they never showed disrespect in that regard. However, I would not dare to excuse them for the inappropriate way in which they acted, and for their lack of good intentions. And it is because of this lack of good intentions that I believe that they failed in all of their undertakings, not only in the sense that they failed to accomplish their goals, but even more so, because they became so entrenched in these activities that, through their fault, innocent and guiltless people were made to suffer with them.

Neither will I, by my silence, give credence to the assertion of those who say, and would have others believe, that they followed the Constable's opinion or the King's will out of fervent loyalty and love. Those who uphold this opinion do so either through ignorance or simple-mindedness. God forbid that I should defame so many noble and great men; I do not. I do not mean to say that they were disloyal or disrespectful to the King. What I do say is that their loyalty was tied up and mixed with great self-interest, so much so that I believe that if you were to remove the possibility of personal gain, or if the spoils taken from the other side were not offered to them, these followers of the King would be better regarded as opportunists and accomplished factionalists than as the rigorous pursuers of justice that they were taken for. Thus, I conclude that, in all truth, although one group's cause may have been more flamboyant and compelling than the other's, the motivating factor was personal gain. So, the absolute truth is that, in this dispute, neither side was right, neither the plaintiffs nor the defendants. The only thing that can be said is that the name of one side was more illustrious, and that that side had a more specious, legitimate, or legitimatized cause, in contrast to the other side. But, as for the King's personal safety and the protection of him and of his crown, I give testimony to God that I never felt or knew that this faction was disrespectful to the King.

I cannot clearly and honestly speak about, or cast judgment on, the Battle of Olmedo, the last and most criminal act, because I was not there. Nor can my opinion exonerate them, because events reached such a point that people were near to losing their estates. In such circumstances, loyalty and justice are often disregarded and break down. You can find very few people who are completely honest and loyal. Only King David is deserving of this praise and glory. Despite King Saul's cruel persecution of him, King David refused to touch him, although on two occasions he had the opportunity to kill him. I have never read of such perfect virtue in any other.

As the *Decretal* states: "The privilege of the few does not make common law."[41] Likewise, one single act does not make a general rule. First of all, they acted because they, themselves, and their estates were in extreme danger; but still, they actually went to battle against the King.

I cannot judge their intentions, but by all appearances, they were not good. If they had won and had taken their revenge on the others, they probably would have respected the King as they had done on previous occasions. But it is not for me to say since, as I have already said, to be absolutely loyal in such extreme danger requires spiritual perfection. In the Book of Kings you can read about the encounter between Joab, David's constable, and Abner,

---

41. A decretal is a letter promulgated by the Pope to resolve a doubt or controversial issue of faith.

Constable of the house of Saul, which took place near the lagoon of Gibeon.[42] When Abner was beaten and saw that Joab was following him, Abner turned to him and said: "Why do you not order your people to stop pursuing their brothers? Do you not know how dangerous desperation is?" And Joab did stop pursuing him, even though Abner had killed Joab's brother, a good knight, in this fight and conflict. Thus, if we choose the most reasonable course, and even judge from past acts, we could conjecture that if these lords had won, they would have respected the King's person as they had done on other occasions. But this is only my opinion, not fact. Yet, by this, I do not want to excuse them of the two things of which I charge them: first, that from the very beginning, their actions were motivated by self-interest, ambition, and greed, not by the desire to provide good order or rule to the Kingdom; second, that the form of their action was twisted and marred by cruelty and scandal, which often spoil the results.

In conclusion, in my opinion, the sins of the Spaniards resulted in all of these evils: first, the negligence and remissness of the King; second, the presumptuousness and daring of a knight to rule and govern over such great Kingdoms and such distinguished people; and third, I must not fail to mention, the avarice of the great knights.

Although we continue to sin, not amending our ways—you could even say our sins are greater in number and are more grave—we beg our Lord that our problems not increase in proportion to our sins, but rather that through His infinite compassion and mercy and through the intercession of his Blessed Mother, He mitigate and soften our punishment, giving good kings to such devout people who may deserve them. It is my considered and thoughtful opinion that neither good times nor good health are as beneficial and necessary to a kingdom as is a just and prudent king, for he is,

---

42. The correct reference for this quote is 2 Samuel II, 25.

after all, the prince of peace. When our Lord left this world, in his last will and testament, his only bequest to us was peace. It is this peace that a good king, with the help of God, can give us. It is not the world that can provide us with peace, but as the Church proclaims: *Quam mundus dare non potest.*[43]

43. See John XIV, 27.

APPENDIX • Personal Titles Used in This Translation

Below is a list of personal titles used in this translation. In parenthesis after each entry is the Spanish title as it appears in the original text. Where appropriate, a description is given of the functions performed by one holding that title in fifteenth-century Castilla.

Admiral *(Almirante)*: Position created in Castilla by Fernando III. The title is defined in the *Siete Partidas* as chief of all warships.

Bishop *(Obispo)*: Church official whose right and duty it was to assure that Church laws were followed in his territory. He was superior to ordained priests and participated in the teaching and administrative functions of the Church.

Chief Justice *(Justicia Mayor)*: Chief judge who represented the king in the royal court. He decided on appeals and ruled on verdicts of other courts and of inferior judges.

Count *(Conde)*: An honorary title below that of the marquis. Titles of nobility were ranked in the following order: prince, duke, marquis, count.

Constable *(Condestable)*: Head of the army. The position was first instituted by Juan I.

Deputy *(Lugarteniente)*: In Aragón, the first dignitary after the monarch with full civil and criminal jurisdiction. He had the power to convoke the *Cortes* and to promulgate laws.

Duke *(Duque)*: A title used to designate the highest rank below that of the prince.

Governor *(Adelantado)*: A provincial governor with military, political, and judicial powers. Originally, the *adelantado* was in charge of the provinces on the frontier with Granada.

Grandees *(Grandes)*: Before the fourteenth and fifteenth centuries they were known as *ricos hombres* (rich men). The title is indicative of old, noble lineage, something the king could not grant, although it was sometimes conferred for some remarkable deed or great service.

Judge *(Alcalde):* Title that designates all officials invested with judicial functions. Prior to the fifteenth century, they may have been elected from the membership of local councils or appointed by a lord of a given estate. By the fifteenth century, they were generally appointed by the king. They had jurisdiction over both civil and criminal matters, but grave offenses were reserved for the judgment of higher authorities.

King (Rey): In Spain, the institution of the monarchy was not absolute. The king was restrained by local laws and by the rights derived from social class. The monarch himself was obliged to follow all laws and not to violate the rights of others. Beginning in the fourteenth century, monarchs began to concentrate power in their hands, moving in the direction of absolute monarchy. The monarch's charges were to rule the kingdom justly, to protect his subjects and their possessions, to ensure peace and territorial integrity, to protect the Church, to take necessary actions to promote the public good, and to provide for punishment of infractions. He had the power to declare war and to negotiate peace treaties. He commanded the army, oversaw the royal treasury, and served as chief administrator of the kingdom.

Knight *(Caballero):* Historically a knight was a person of noble ancestry, but later the title was granted to those who did battle on their own horse and at their own expense. Knights were members of the lesser nobility.

Lord *(Señor):* Anyone who exercised any power or authority over others or over a particular region, often the owner of a large tract of land holding power over its inhabitants. In some cases, the king granted the lord special priviledges and immunities and the right to carry out certain functions of the State within his territory.

Marquis *(Marqués):* Title of nobility between duke and count.

Marshal *(Mariscal):* High military official.

Master *(Maestre):* Master of one of the military orders.

Representative *(Procurador):* Representative of the town to the *Cortes* (see Introduction Footnote 3).

Royal Chaplain *(Capellán Mayor):* Official in charge of the royal chapel, part of the household, or court of the king. The royal chaplain was always a bishop who served as royal confessor and performed the offices on great religious feast days.

Royal Chamberlain *(Camarero Mayor)*: One of a group of intimate friends and counselors who surrounded medieval monarchs. Their titles came from the time when each was assigned a special role in the managing of the monarch's household. They still theoretically had these duties but also held administrative and secretarial offices related to the governing of the kingdom. The royal chamberlain was head of the palace and was in charge of the general direction of palace services, the administration of the king's house, and the royal treasury and domains.

Royal Chancellor *(Canciller Mayor)*: Most often a cleric whose duty it was to oversee royal correspondence and the promulgation of royal orders. The king's decrees required the chancellor's signature to insure their validity. The chancellor was keeper of the royal seal.

Royal Notary *(Notario Mayor)*: Subordinate of the royal chancellor.

Royal steward *(Mayordomo)*: See Royal Chamberlain.

Royal tax collector *(Contador Mayor)*: Tax gatherer for the king and customhouse officer.

WORKS CONSULTED

Adams, Nicholson B., and John E. Keller. *Breve panorama de la literatura española.* Trans. Antonio Llorente Maldonado de Guevara. Madrid: Castalia, 1964.

Bordona, Domínguez, ed. *Generaciones y Semblanzas,* by Fernán Pérez de Guzmán. Madrid: Espasa-Calpe, 1924.

de la Cierva, Ricardo. *Historia General de España: Baja edad media: Predominio cristiano.* Vol. 4. Madrid: Planeta, 1981.

Deyermond, A. D. *A Literary History of Spain: The Middle Ages.* New York: Barnes and Noble, 1971.

―――. *La literatura perdida de la Edad Media castellana: Catalago y estudio I Epica y romances.* Salamanca: Ediciones Universitarias de Salamanca, 1995.

Diccionario de historia de España desde sus orígenes hasta el fin del Reinado de Alfonso XIII. Madrid: Revista de Occidente, 1952.

Harrison, Lucia. "Un poeta a caballo entre dos siglos: Fernán Pérez de Guzmán." In the *Online Resource Book for Medieval Studies* (ORB), 1997. [cited 21 September 1999]. Available from <http://orb.rhodes.edu/encyclop/culture/lit/Spanish/perez_de_guzman.html>.

Highfield, Roger, ed. *Spain in the Fifteenth Century, 1369–1516.* Trans. Frances M. López-Morillas. London: Macmillan Press, 1972.

Jackson, Gabriel. *Making of Medieval Spain.* Norwich: Harcourt, Brace, Jovanovich, Inc., 1972.

Menéndez Pidal, Ramón. *Historia de España: Los Trastámaras de Castilla y Aragón en el siglo XV.* Vol. 15. Madrid: Espasa-Calpe, 1964.

Merriman, Roger Bigelow. *The Rise of the Spanish Empire in the Old World and in the New: The Middle Ages.* Vol. 1. New York: Cooper Square Publishers, 1962.

O'Callaghan, Joseph F. *A History of Medieval Spain.* Ithaca: Cornell University Press, 1975.

Pulgar, Fernando del. *Claros Varones de Castilla.* Ed. R. B. Tate. London: Oxford University Press, 1971.

Russell, P. E., ed. *Spain: A Companion to Spanish Studies.* London: Methuen and Co, 1973.

Suárez Fernández, Luis, coordinator. *Historia General de España y América: Los Trastámaras y la Unidad Española 1369–1517.* Vol. 5. Madrid: Ediciones Rialp, 1981.

Tate, R. B., ed. *Generaciones y Semblanzas,* by Fernán Pérez de Guzmán. London: Tamesis, 1965.

Weiss, Julian. "Fernán Pérez de Guzmán: Poet in Exile." In *Speculum* 66 (January, 1991): 96–108.

INDEX OF PERSONS MENTIONED IN THE TEXT

Abner, 72, 73
Alfonso, Bishop of Burgos. *See* García de Santa María, Alfonso
Alfonso, Marqués de Villena, 18, 44
Alfonso IV, father of Don Fadrique, 19
Alfonso V. *See* Alfonso de Aragón, son of Fernando I
Alfonso VI, father of Queen Urraca, 23
Alfonso VII, son of Queen Urraca, 23
Alfonso XI, 49
Alfonso de Aragón, husband of Queen Urraca, 23
Alfonso de Aragón, son of Fernando I, 17
Álvarez de Asturias, Rodrigo, 35
Álvarez Osorio, Garci, 11
Álvarez de Toledo, Fernán, 67
Álvarez de Toledo, María, 36
Arias de Balboa, Vicente, 29
Arista, Íñigo, 22
Asuero, King of Persia, 25
Augustine, St., 59
Ayala, Aldonza de, 22
Ayala, Leonor de, 36

Barientos, Lope de, 58
Benavides, Gómez de, 67
Benedict XIII. *See* Luna, Pedro de
Benevente, Count of. *See* Pimentel, Rodrigo Alonso de
Benevente, Duke of. *See* Fadrique
Boethius, 21

Campo de Espina, Gómez, 23
Catalina, wife of Prince Enrique of Aragón, 12
Catalina of Lancaster, Queen of Castilla, 12, 14, 47, 51, 52, 57
Chrysostom, St. John, 3
Cid Ali, 16
Cid Ruy Díaz, 22
Cidi Hamete, 16
Colonne, Guido delle, 7
Constable. *See* Luna, Álvaro de
Corral, Pedro de, 3
Costanza, daughter of Pedro I of Castilla, 12
Costanza de Tovar, 19
Cuello, Egas, 10

Dávalos, Alfonso, 11
David, King, 14, 72

Edward III, 12
Enrique, Prince of Aragón, 12, 17, 58
Enrique, Prince of Asturias (Enrique IV), 61, 69
Enrique II, 20, 33, 50, 51, 57, 61, 68
Enrique III, 3, 7–12, 13, 18, 21, 23, 26, 29, 33, 40
Enríquez, Alfonso, 19–20, 57, 58

81

82 INDEX

Enríquez, Enrique, 67
Enríquez, Fadrique, Admiral of Castilla, 67, 68
Enríquez, Fadrique, Count of Trastámara, 67
Esquierdo, King of the Moors, 43

Fabricio, 48
Fadrique, Admiral of Castilla. *See* Enríquez Fadrique
Fadrique, Count of Luna, 67
Fadrique, Count of Trastámara. *See* Enríquez, Fadrique
Fadrique, Duke of Benevente, 26
Fadrique, Master of Santiago, 18, 19
Fernández Coronel, Alfonso, 49
Fernández de Córdoba, Diego, 34
Fernández de Quiñones, Diego, 35–36
Fernández de Velasco, Pedro, Count of Haro, 69
Fernández de Velasco, Pedro, Royal Chamberlain of Enrique II, 27
Fernández Pacheco, Juan, 10
Fernández Pacheco, Lope, 10
Fernando I, 11, 12–17, 28, 38, 51, 52, 53, 57, 58
Fernando III, 8
Ferrández, Garci, 27
Ferrández Manrique, García, 68
Florentina, St., 7
Frías, Pedro de, 50–51
Fulgentius, St., 7

García de Santa María, Alfonso, 41, 43
García de Santa María, Alvar, 6
García de Santa María, Pablo, Bishop of Burgos, 39–43
García Manrique, Juan, 26–27
Gómez de Campo de Espina, 23
Gómez de Sandoval, Diego, 38–39
Gómez de Toledo, Gutierre, 46, 67, 69
González de Avellaneda, Juan, 32
González de Camelo, Alvar, 10

González de Herrera, Garci, 9, 33
González de Mendoza, Pedro, 22
González, Fernán, 27
Gonzalo, Bishop of Plasencia, 43
Gonzalo, Bishop of Segovia, 29
Goodman, Duke of Brittany, 24
Gregory, St., 21
Guivara, Elvira de, 19
Guzmán, Juan Alfonso de, 30
Guzmán, Leonor de, 49

Haro, Count of. *See* Fernández de Velasco, Pedro
Hermenegild, 8
Herod, King, 25
Herrera, Juan de, 11
Hurtado de Mendoza, Diego, 10, 22–23, 33, 68
Hurtado de Mendoza, Fernando, 23
Hurtado de Mendoza, Juan, 33

Illescas, Gonzalo de, 58
Illescas, Juan de, 29, 52
Isabel, daughter of Juan II, 61
Isidore, St., 7, 21

Joab, 72, 73
John of Lancaster, 12
Juan, Prince of Aragón and King of Navarra, 17, 38, 39, 58, 60
Juan I, King of Castilla, 18, 20, 21, 29
Juan I, King of Portugal, 9, 27
Juan II, 3, 11, 13, 37, 42, 51–61, 62
Juana, illegitimate daughter of Enrique II, 44
Julián, Count, 42, 48

Lara, Pedro de, 23, 26
Leander, St., 7
Leonor, daughter of Pedro IV of Aragón, 7, 53
Leonor, sister of the princes of Aragón, 17

INDEX 83

Livy, 21
López, Fernando, 47
López Dávalos, Ruy, 10, 11, 17–19, 50, 51, 57, 58, 67, 68
López de Ayala, Pedro, 20–21
López de Córdoba, Leonor, 47
López de Mendoza, Iñigo, Marquis of Santillana, 69
López de Saldaña, Fernán, 67
López de Stúñiga, Diego, 10, 21–22, 50, 51, 52
Luna, Álvaro de, 49, 55–61, 62–74
Luna, Álvaro de, the Elder, 62
Luna, Juan Mate de, 44
Luna, Pedro de, Archbishop of Toledo, 62
Luna, Pedro de, Benedict XIII, 40, 62

Madrid, Juan Alfonso de, 29
Manrique, Count of Lara, 26
Manrique, Gómez, 30–31, 50
Manrique, Pedro, 37–38, 57, 58, 67, 68, 69
Manrique, Pedro, the Elder, 30
María, daughter of Fernando de Aragón, 17, 58
María, wife of Alfonso V of Aragón, 11
Martín, King of Aragón, 16, 53
Martín II, King of Sicily, 16
Martínez de Rojas, Juan, 28
Mendoza, Juana de, 37
Mendoza, Lope de, 43–44
Metellus, 4

Narbáez, Rodrigo de, 16
Niño, Pero, 67
Núñez de Guzmán, Gonzalo, 10, 24–26, 30

Ocrato, Prior of, 10
Ortiz de Stúñiga, Lope, 16

Padilla, María de, 12
Pedro, Count of Lara, 23, 26
Pedro, Count of Trastámara, 18, 49
Pedro, father of Enrique de Villena, 44
Pedro, King of Aragón, 7, 18
Pedro, King of Castilla, 19, 20, 21, 49
Pedro, Prince of Aragón, son of Fernando I, 17
Pedro, Prince of Aragón and father of Don Alfonso, Marqués de Villena, 18
Pérez de Ayala, Fernán, 20
Pérez de Guzmán, Alvar, 11
Pérez de Guzmán, Fernán, 67
Pérez de Osorio, Álvar, 34
Pérez de Vivero, Alonso, 60, 69
Pimentel, Rodrigo Alonso de, 69

Quiñones, Pedro, 67
Quiñones, Suero de, 67

Ramiro, Count, 24
Recaredo, 7
Ribera, Pedro Afán de, 32–33
Robles, Fernán Alonso de, 46–49, 67
Rodrigo, 42, 48
Rojas, Lope de, 67
Rojas, María de, 28
Rojas, Martín de, 11
Rojas, Sancho de, 11, 16, 28, 38, 51, 57

Sánchez d'Alvarado, Garci, 67
Sánchez de Benavides, Día, 11
Sancho, Count of Alburquerque, 33
Sancho, Prince of Aragón, 17
Saul, King, 14, 72, 73
Scipio, 4
Solomon, King, 54
Sotomayor, Juan de, 67
Stúñiga, Álvaro de, 60
Stúñiga, Pedro de, Count of Placensia, 69

Suárez de Figueróa, Lorenzo, 31–32
Suárez de Quiñones, Pedro, 10, 35–36

Tenorio, Pedro, 26, 28
Teodosia, St., 8
Tolosa, Ramón de, 23
Tordesillas, Juan de, 50

Urraca, Queen, 23

Vadillo, Diego de, 67
Vázquez de Acuña, Gil, 10
Vázquez de Acuña, Lope, 10
Vázquez de Acuña, Martín, 10
Velasco, Juan de, 16, 27–28, 50, 51, 52, 57
Villena, Enrique de, 44–46

Witiza, 48